100 QUESTIONS JESUS ASKED

100 QUESTIONS JESUS ASKED

by Janet E. Reinhard

Publishing House
St. Louis

Library of Congress Cataloging in Publication Data

Reinhard, Janet E., 1920-
100 questions Jesus asked.

1. Jesus Christ—Words—Meditations. I. Title.
BT306.R39   232.9'54   81-12538
ISBN 0-570-03841-3   AACR2

1 2 3 4 5 6 7 8 9 10 MAL 91 90 89 88 87 86 85 84 83 82

To   the memory of Gerhard Belgum,
       who encouraged and supported;
     my friend Leslie Brandt,
       whose enthusiasm opened doors;
     my husband Karl,
       who never doubted;
     all of God's children—everywhere—
       who assume the responsibility of
       GRACE
       in discipleship.

Contents

Foreword

Gertrude Stein, on her deathbed, was asked by her lifelong companion Alice B. Toklas for a summary of life from the vantage point of hindsight: "What is the answer, Gertrude?" To which Miss Stein responded, "What's the question?"

Many, many people have found the Answer to their most basic and troubling questions to be Jesus Christ. Just as many—and more—have not found the answer, because they have not been asking the right questions.

No one who reads the gospels can miss the questioning Christ. A dinner speaker in Minneapolis several years ago provided the seed for this book by making the passing statement that Jesus asked 100 questions. Our tabulation of the questions sticking like barbs in the fields of Christ's discourses came up with even more than 100, not counting some duplications.

Janet Reinhard was fascinated by the subject and in her contemplation of the questions searched out the setting for each of them and proposed some personal reactions. These responses are by no means everyone's reverberation to the nagging questions of earth's heavenly Visitor and future Judge. Those who heard them the first time were obliged to render an answer or, if they turned away speechless, they were to know that the questions would not go away but would demand an answer in the final confrontation with the One whom God appointed to be Savior and Final Reckoner.

The
Kingdom
of God

Can the wedding guests mourn as long as the bridegroom is with them?

Matthew 9:15

In the Jewish family a wedding was a time of abundant joy, enthusiastic merriment, and happy sharing—a celebration of pure rejoicing. For the poor people it was probably the only really festive occasion of their lives—seven days of laughter and music, dancing and feasting. Guests were exempt from religious obligations; they did not have to fast. (Strict Jews fasted Mondays and Thursdays.)

When a son reached the age of marrying—usually about 20 years old—his parents looked for a suitable bride among the families of their village. After a bride was found, the fathers of the young people negotiated a wedding agreement; a *mohar* or dowry was paid to the bride's father by the groom and his father.

On the first day of the wedding celebration—in their respective homes—the bride and groom were adorned with "crowns," headbands of gold or silver, or a wreath of flowers. They were treated like a king and a queen. Their attendants, groomsmen or bridesmaids, carried out their every wish and whim. When everything was in readiness, a procession of bridegroom, groomsmen, family, and friends went to the home of the bride to escort her party to the home of the bridegroom's father, where the wedding festivities took place. They were a joyous band of people, singing and dancing and merrymaking. It was also a time of transition for the bride—she left the authority of her father to become the property of her husband. The bridegroom became her lord and master.

Early in Jesus' ministry the disciples of John the Baptist came to Him inquiring: "Why do we and the Pharisees fast, but your disciples do not fast?" He answered them with a little parable about a wedding: "Can the wedding guests mourn as long as the bridegroom is with them?"

Jesus came to usher in the kingdom of God. The kingdom of God is often compared to a wedding. Jesus is the Bridegroom, the King, come to claim His bride, the church. The bride, all humankind, has been chosen by the Father. The dowry the Father paid is His dearly beloved Son. The Father's house is the kingdom of God. The coming of Jesus is indeed cause for rejoicing and celebration for all His disciples—the groomsmen—then and now and down through the ages to come!

Matthew 9:14-15; 25:1-13; Mark 2:18-20;
Luke 5:33-35; John 2:1-11

What kind of attitudes are betrayed by fasting and mourning in the presence of our living Savior—the Bridegroom? How can we celebrate in the kingdom of God now?

═══

What do you seek? . . .
So you are Simon the son of John?
John 1:38, 42

Most of us are seekers—of peace of mind, blessedness, enlightenment, fulfillment, happiness. There are those who do not know what they are seeking. But they do know that their lives are empty, without purpose.

Andrew and an unnamed friend were seekers. They were disciples of John the Baptist during his short but fervent mission. To the many Jews waiting and hoping for the coming Messiah, John announced the fulfillment of their hope: "Behold, the Lamb of God who takes away the sin of the world!" (Lamb of God is synonymous with Messiah.)

One day when John was standing with Andrew and the unnamed disciple, he saw Jesus walking by and said, "Behold, the Lamb of God!" The two immediately left John and followed Jesus. To His question, "What do you seek?" they replied, "Rabbi, where are You staying?" Jesus' reply, "Come and see," was a call to discipleship in the kingdom of God. The Bible does not record the dialog between Jesus and the two disciples. However, we do know that they responded to Jesus' call; they knew that He was the Messiah.

Early the next morning Andrew went looking for his brother Simon to tell him: "We have found the Messiah." Eagerly he took him to Jesus, whose greeting was: "So you are Simon the son of John? You shall be called Cephas" (which means Peter). Jesus' call to discipleship with its emphasis on a new name—Simon to Peter—reflects the experience of the patriarchs when they encountered God and accepted His call: Jacob became Israel, Abram became Abraham. Simon, too, had encountered God but in the new age of the kingdom of God in the person of the Messiah!

13

Jesus still calls those who seek—even when they do not know what it is they seek. When we come to the realization that Jesus is asking, "Whom do you seek?" rather than, "What do you seek?" we, too, will have found the Messiah as Andrew did. For those who are called—and who accept their role of discipleship in the kingdom of God—their mission is to bring other seekers to the kingdom of God. And there, by the unending grace of God, they find reconciliation and peace, harmony with God.

John 1:29-42; Mark 1:16-20; Luke 5:1-11

How do you know that you have found the Messiah? Did you really find Him, or did He find you?

Because I said to you, I saw you under the fig tree, do you believe?

John 1:50

The leaves of the fig tree are large and thick, and in the summertime they form a cool, green canopy to shade one from the intense heat of the sun. In the Old Testament the fig tree was a symbol of shelter and peace—the peace of the Messianic kingdom of God, reconciliation to and harmony with God. A Jew was blessed, indeed, who had his own fig tree under whose branches he could rest and meditate undisturbed.

Nathanael sat under his fig tree in prayer and contemplation. He was a devout man, faithful to the Law and the Prophets, filled with hope of the Messiah who was to come. He knew the prophecies well, and he longed for their fulfillment.

But Nathanael, though a deeply religious man, was also a skeptical person, and stubborn too. When Philip came to him saying, "We have found Him of whom Moses in the law and also the prophets wrote, Jesus of Nazareth, the son of Joseph," Nathanael ridiculed him. Nazareth was nothing but a small, backward village! How could the Messiah possibly come from such a place? But he did go along with Philip to see for himself.

When Jesus saw Nathanael coming to Him, He said, "Behold, an Israelite indeed, in whom is no guile." Nathanael was astonished that

Jesus knew him. Jesus' explanation was even more astounding: "Before Philip called you, when you were under the fig tree, I saw you." Immediately, Nathanael perceived what the leaders of Israel failed to see—that Jesus was the Messiah, the Son of God, the King of Israel. Spiritual Israel, the Messianic kingdom of God, had broken into history!

Jesus' question: "Because I said to you, I saw you under the fig tree, do you believe?" has tremendous implication for us. Nathanael easily understood the Messianic reference in the fig tree. The symbolism of the fig tree comes to us in Word and sacrament—and in the witness of faithful Christians who ask us to "Come and see." And even more in the steadfast love of our Savior who, knowing our strengths and weaknesses, never stops calling us. But sometimes, unlike Nathanael, we do not see or hear or respond. It is only when we are confronted with the power of our crucified and resurrected Savior—His Spirit of truth and understanding—that we perceive that He knows us for what we are, that He loves us as we are, and that only He has the power to call, to change, and to direct us. He gives us faith and power to serve in His kingdom!

John 1:43-51; 1 Kings 4:25; Psalm 32:2; Micah 4:1-4; Zechariah 3:10

Why do you believe? Do you think it is possible to analyze it?

Do you not understand this parable? How then will you understand all the parables?

Mark 4:13

Jesus had many ways of teaching: the love and concern which He showed for widows and children, the poor and outcasts; His healing of those with physical handicaps or illness of mind and body; His profound and eloquent sermons in the synagogues; His discourse and rebuttal to the learned rabbis, priests, and Pharisees; the parables He used to teach great crowds of people who gathered on hillsides and by the sea.

The parables were simple, down-to-earth accounts of everyday, ordinary things that had deep spiritual meaning. They were spoken stories whose intent was to make each one think and reflect about his faith in God, to help each one understand the truth about his own relationship to God, and to point out each one's responsibility in the kingdom of God.

There were many people who listened to the parables, but only a relatively few understood their meaning. It was not because of indifference to Jesus' message or even opposition to His ministry. It was simply that, after years and years of Roman oppression, persecution, and religious separatism, the idea of a Messiah to the great majority of Jews was that of a great political leader who would restore a secular nation, Israel.

To the disciples had been given the "secret of the kingdom of God"—that the kingdom of God had entered history through the incarnation and ministry of Jesus. It could be understood only by those who perceived their need for Jesus as Savior and Lord of their lives, who knew forgiveness, and therefore wanted to serve in His kingdom.

Those disciples, then and now, who begin to understand can acquire more insight through faithful listening, study, prayer, dialog, meditation, and self-sacrifice—"more will be given, and he will have abundance." Those who are lazy and indifferent are in danger of losing what they now understand—"even what he has will be taken away." Temptation, indifference, pride, persecution, the pull of secularism, materialism—these will cause some disciples to fall away. But as in the parable, even though some seed is wasted, there will be an abundant harvest. God never stops calling His beloved children to repentance and forgiveness; His message is not hidden.

Mark 4:1-20; Matthew 13:1-23; Luke 8:4-15; Deuteronomy 29:4; Isaiah 6:9-10; Jeremiah 5:21; Ezekiel 12:2

How would you interpret the parable for today?

With what can we compare the kingdom of God, or what parable shall we use for it?
Mark 4:30

In the Old Testament a tree was often used as a symbol of a large empire which gave shelter, protection, and security to the people of the small nations over which it had dominion. For instance, in Daniel 4:20-22 the tree in the king's dream refers to King Nebuchadnezzar himself; the birds are the small nations within this vast kingdom.

When Jesus answered His own question with the parable of the Mustard Seed, this could, therefore, be understood in the light of the Old Testament Scriptures. When Daniel interpreted another dream of King Nebuchadnezzar, these were his words: "And in the days of those kings the God of heaven will set up a kingdom which shall never be destroyed." The king himself said about our God: "His kingdom is an everlasting kingdom, and His dominion is from generation to generation." A later king, Darius, said: "He is the living God, enduring forever; His kingdom shall never be destroyed, and His dominion shall be to the end."

The kingdom of God has not been destroyed—and it will never be destroyed! It will continue to exist throughout eternity! Like the tiny mustard seed, it has grown from a small band of struggling disciples to a universal kingdom, embracing the whole world. It is like the flourishing shade tree which shelters the birds who nest in it from the howling winds of storms and the merciless heat of the desert sun. But, unlike the empire it symbolized in the time of Nebuchadnezzar, it is a spiritual kingdom whose shelter is God's steadfast, unending love and grace and forgiveness. It is ruled by One who protects us in time of danger and guards us from all evil, who gave His Son in self-sacrifice so that we might live in that kingdom to serve Him in peace and harmony, and who sent His Holy Spirit to enlighten us with His gifts and to keep us in true and abiding faith.

Mark 4:30-32; Matthew 13:31-32; Luke 13:18-19; Daniel 2:44; 4:1-37; 6:25-28

How do you perceive the kingdom of God? How exclusive and inclusive is it?

Have you understood all this?
Matthew 13:51

"Yes," replied the disciples to Jesus' question. We wonder if they really did—anymore than we do, who have the advantage of 2,000 years of study, interpretation, and teaching. There is still much that remains a mystery in the kingdom of God. The one thing that we really and truly understand—or should—is that each of us is a responsible servant in the kingdom. The lives of the disciples show that self-concern, pride, persecution, ostracism, and humiliation can impede mission, but they also show the renewing power of the Spirit of God.

In the time of Jesus the scribe was the interpreter of Sacred Scripture. He was a teacher, expert in the law of Moses. He had a great deal of authority and, like people since the beginning of time, he could be vain and prideful. He allowed rules of behavior to obscure God's message of love and care.

The Christian who seeks to understand must find in the Old Testament not so much its laws but rather its beautiful messages of grace and love and hope. Grace jumps up at us from Genesis through Malachi! It is the precious treasure of the householder who brings out "what is old" to enhance and complement the new; it reveals the secret of the Kingdom, God's will that everyone be saved. Its prophecies of hope for the eventual kingdom of God are indescribably moving and sublime—and fulfilled for us in Christ.

But the New Testament is now old—in its second millennium of existence—and legalistic minds have ever been trying to turn the Gospel of grace into a code of conduct. Rather than seeking new insights and contemporary challenge, the legalists in our midst promulgate rules and obscure grace.

Jesus admonishes us: "The scribes and the Pharisees sit on Moses' seat; so practice and observe whatever they tell you, but not what they do; for they preach but do not practice. . . . Woe to you, scribes and Pharisees, hypocrites! because you shut the kingdom of heaven against men; for you neither enter yourselves, nor allow those who would enter to go in." We must be open to the Spirit to fuse the old with what is of value in the new, so that we may witness to the kingdom of God in this time to everyone, everywhere!

Matthew 13:51-52; 23:1-36

In light of Jesus' pronouncement, "The kingdom of God is at hand; repent and believe in the Gospel" (Mark 1:15), do you perceive Jesus' mission and your own in that kingdom?

Now which of them will love him more? . . .
Do you see this woman?

Luke 7:42, 44

Simon, a Pharisee, once invited Jesus to dinner. It was the custom of the Oriental well-to-do elite to allow the door to the courtyard where dinner was served to remain open. Intellectuals could, therefore, come to hear pearls of wisdom from the learned men assembled at the table; beggars could enter, hoping for some scraps of food; anyone at all could stop by.

As a sign of respect, the invited guest was accorded three courtesies: the kiss of peace, cool water for cleansing his feet, and perfumed oil to anoint his head. For some reason Simon declined to extend these courtesies to Jesus.

At an Oriental dinner table the guests reclined on a couch on one elbow with their feet extended behind them. A woman who probably had seen and heard Jesus teach earlier and who was aware that He was in Simon's house came into the courtyard. Weeping, she cleansed Jesus' feet with her tears, wiped them with her hair and kissed them, and anointed them with precious perfume from an alabaster vial which she wore around her neck.

Simon was appalled; he saw the woman only as a sinner of bad reputation. He would never have allowed her to touch him, for he then would have been ritually unclean, contaminated by her sinfulness. But Jesus saw the woman as a person aware of her sin and of her forgiveness.

"Now which of them will love him more?"—the question Jesus asked of Simon was to force him to think about forgiveness in the light of His little story about two debtors who were forgiven their debts. One owed 50 denarii; the other owed 500 denarii. (One denarius was equal to one day's wages for a laborer.) The story had tremendous significance for Simon, as it does for us today. Simon was so concerned with the woman's sinfulness that he failed to see that he, too, was a sinner in need of forgiveness. Even in the presence of the compassionate, Holy One of God, he was unable to forgive. Pharisees often did not perceive—nor did they want to—that forgiveness was for everyone and that all persons are in need of it.

"Do you see this woman? . . . Her sins, which are many, are forgiven, for she loved much." Jesus' question and benediction

19

applies to each and every one of us—we are sinners and saints alike in the kingdom of God.

Luke 7:36-50

Is there a little bit of the Pharisee in each of us? How is it manifested? How can we overcome it?

Do you not say, "There are yet four months, then comes the harvest"?
John 4:35

Jesus and His disciples were on their way from Judea to Galilee. The long, dusty journey took them through Samaria, where Jesus stopped by Jacob's well outside of the city of Sychar to rest. His disciples left Him to go search for food.

While He rested at the well, a Samaritan woman came to draw water. Samaritans were generally despised as infidels, not worthy to be called Jews. But Jesus spoke to her, and in the conversation that followed He revealed that He was the Messiah. "I who speak to you am He." She immediately left Him to return to the city with her good news—she believed!

When the disciples returned with food, they were shocked at Jesus' action but they did not question Him. The rabbis taught that a man should not speak to a woman on the street, not even his wife. Jesus was not bound by the traditions of the rabbis. His mission was to bring God's love and forgiveness to all people—Jew, Samaritan, and Gentile, male and female.

When the disciples offered Him food, Jesus said to them: "I have food to eat of which you do not know . . . My food is to do the will of Him who sent Me, and to accomplish His work." He explained with a simple little Hebrew parable: "Do you not say, 'There are yet four months, then comes the harvest'?"

In the Old Testament harvest is the symbol of the last judgment which brings eternal life in the kingdom of God to those who believe. Jesus was speaking of a spiritual harvest—the Jews to whom He brought love and forgiveness, the Samaritans to whom the woman would bring the good news of the Messiah, and the Gentiles to whom the disciples would carry the glorious news of the resurrection! The kingdom of God was not to be the exclusive dominion of the Jews. The fields were ripe all around, ready for the harvest. Jesus was willing to give His life to accomplish it.

Sometimes the disciple who sows the seed of God's love and forgiveness never sees the harvest of his labor. The time is short! There is a place in God's kingdom for every talent, and none is without value. Jesus' work must now become our work in mission.

The fields are still white, ready for the harvest. Today there are masses of people everywhere—all waiting for the harvest!

John 4:3-42

Where do you see the fields ready for harvest? What can you do to help?

Are you a teacher of Israel, and yet you do not understand this? . . . If I have told you earthly things and you do not believe, how can you believe if I tell you heavenly things?

John 6:10, 12

Nicodemus was a learned Pharisee, a member of the Sanhedrin. The Sanhedrin was a court of civil and religious law—the final authority in the interpretation of the Mosaic law. One must assume, then, that Nicodemus was well versed in Old Testament Scripture. He came at night to see Jesus, perhaps because he did not want to be seen by fellow Pharisees, or because the likelihood of undisturbed conversation was far greater at night than during the day. He recognized Jesus as a man of God; great prophets were often known by the signs they accomplished. Nicodemus wanted to know more about Jesus and what He taught.

But he could not accept Jesus' first words, "Truly, truly, I say to you, unless one is born anew, he cannot see the kingdom of God," or the ones that followed, "Unless one is born of water and the Spirit, he cannot enter the kingdom of God." Could it be that his literal interpretation of Jesus' words, his lack of understanding of these new spiritual concepts, indicated that he really did not want to know the truth? Could it be that he was actually resisting—as so many people did then and still do today—the Gospel that Jesus was proclaiming?

To be born again means to be born from above, spiritual rebirth, new creation from God. It means to receive the Holy Spirit in Baptism, to be born of the water of Baptism and the Word of the Spirit. Baptism is not a magical rite, nor just an external cleansing. It is a "washing of regeneration." Its benefit is appropriated by faith. The new life needs to be nurtured with the pure "milk of the Word."

The Holy Spirit can be resisted and turned away. There are people who feel no need for rebirth—who actually scoff at such a purely spiritual concept, who deny that they need a Savior. But Jesus' words are as valid today as they were 2,000 years ago. To be reconciled to God, to be born again, is the miracle of God's steadfast love and grace.

John 3:1-21; Mark 16:15 f.; Romans 6:1-11; Titus 3:3-7

Why do you think there is so much misunderstanding about Baptism today? How does regeneration resemble natural birth?

You hypocrites! You know how to interpret the appearance of earth and sky; but why do you not know how to interpret the present time? And why do you not judge for yourselves what is right?

Luke 12:56-57

In Palestine winds blowing from the sea brought rain; the Sirocco winds from the desert were hot, dry, and scorching. The hot, dry Santa Ana winds in California scorch the earth and increase the threat of brush and forest fires. The appearance of the sky forewarns the approach of a violent thunderstorm, hurricane, or tornado. The changes in earth or sky are fairly easy to interpret today, as they were in Palestine 2,000 years ago.

More difficult to interpret are the interrelated social, political, and spiritual signs of the time. The signs of destructive and exploitative forces were the same in Jesus' time as they are now: greed, injustice, uneven distribution of natural resources, abuse of power, apathy, self-seeking, perversion of government and relgion. The signs of positive forces are the same: God's constant call to repentance, the response of people in faith to service in the kingdom of God, their sensitivity to the needs of others, their concern for the spiritual and physical welfare of all humankind, their responsible care of the creation.

In its own way Israel was blind to the "present time." The multitudes saw the miracles and signs which announced that the kingdom of God had come. But many of them failed to read those signs.

Jesus knew and understood His Father's will for Himself in the redemption of all humanity. He could also interpret the political and social winds of the time. Rome was a great and powerful nation. Local insurrection against its mighty legions would end in disaster. The Jews were fragmented politically and spiritually, the masses swayed by leaders who were serving their own interests. Rome would tolerate no rebellion.

Israel needed to repent of its national and spiritual pride, to be reconciled to God, to become the people of His kingdom. Israel's denial of God's will would inevitably lead to God's judgment. How little time there was for repentance!

Luke 12:54-59; Matthew 16:1-4

How do we read the signs of our times in terms of the urgency for us to be committed disciples, to take seriously the Great Commission, and to see our obligation to the needy, starving, and suffering people of our planet?

In My Father's house are many rooms; if it were not so, would I have told you that I go to prepare a place for you?
John 14:2

Jesus knew that His time had come. He and His disciples were gathered in an upper room for their last supper together. It was a scene charged with emotion. Jesus had to tell His disciples that He was leaving them: "Where I am going you cannot come" (John 13:33). They were deeply distressed, unable to comprehend the implication of His words. He had revealed to them that one of them would betray Him to the authorities, and that Peter would deny that he had ever known Jesus. They were sick at heart, worried and anxious about losing their Friend and Master—that is, all except Judas, who had been captivated by greed. His soul-searching remorse would come later.

Jesus responded to His sorrowing disciples with loving concern and compassion. "Let not your hearts be troubled; believe in God, believe also in Me." They must trust Jesus more than ever before. It was necessary that He leave them in order to prepare the way for their entrance into the eternal kingdom of God. His promise is phrased in poetic beauty: "In My Father's house are many rooms; if it were not so, would I have told you that I go to prepare a place for you?"

It was commonly believed that there were various places in heaven; one entered a specific place depending on how good he had been in his earthly life. But Jesus was saying that by His going to die on the cross, the way would be opened for everyone to live with Him forever in the kingdom of His Father. "I am the Way, and the Truth, and the Life; no one comes to the Father but by Me."

Jesus assures us of God's eternal love. We are not loved because we are good but because we believe in the One whom God has sent—and in His work in self-offering. Our work during our sojourn in God's kingdom on earth is the obedience of faith—faith which trusts in Jesus' promise of a "place for you" in His Father's eternal kingdom. It is faith which anticipates our eternal dwelling place with God in the peace which passes all understanding, in righteousness and harmony forever! It is faith which cannot be jealously hoarded but, in gratitude to God's love and forgiveness, must be shared openly and unashamedly with all of God's children. The joy and the peace and the beauty of the "Father's house" are for all who believe!

John 14:1-7

What is your idea of eternity? Can we really know what God's eternal kingdom is like? How can we be sure of getting there?

Is this what you are asking yourselves, what I meant by saying, "A little while, and you will not see Me, and again a little while, and you will see Me"?

John 16:19

The disciples were perplexed; they had not the remotest idea of what Jesus meant when He said: "A little while and you will see Me no more; again a little while, and you will see Me." Jesus knew that they were in a quandary. Therefore He tried to explain what was about to happen.

In the gospel of John "world" means the masses of humankind who are blind to the Gospel which Jesus taught in Word and deed, hostile to Jesus and His teaching, unmindful of the prophecies of Scripture, and who consequently have rejected both the Son of God and His kingdom. The figure of a "woman in travail" in Old Testament Scripture personified the coming of the Messianic community, the kingdom of God, a new people.

When Jesus told His disciples that they would be sorrowful while the world rejoiced, He was describing their reaction to His crucifixion, as well as that of those who wanted to see Him put to death. The high priest, the Sanhedrin, the priests and the Pharisees would be relieved to see Him gone; no longer would they have to fear the effect Jesus had on the common, ordinary people. No longer would He be a threat to their security. There would be no danger of revolution. The people themselves would reverse their allegiance and cry, "Crucify! Crucify!" The world would rejoice.

But there was much more to come. "In a little while," after the resurrection, His followers would be overjoyed to see Him again. The tables would be turned! Those who had plotted against Jesus would be confronted with a joyful band of disciples zealous to carry out His mission, inspired by the Holy Spirit to do the will of the Father.

"A little while" also refers to the Second Advent of Jesus, when He will come to judge the world. He will find the world much the same as when He left. There are innumerable disciples working to bring more of God's beloved children into His kingdom. At the same time countless people are rejecting Jesus and His Gospel, and the work of the Holy Spirit. Greed, concern with acquiring money and property at the expense of others, the despoiling of our bountiful creation, insensitivity to the needs of the homeless and starving, denial of human rights and dignity, rampant crime, neglect of justice, and, most of all, pride which refuses to acknowledge one's disharmony with God—these are the signs of a world not at all affected by the warning of the judgment to come. For such a world, rejoicing will turn to sorrow; for disciples, sorrow will turn to rejoicing in God's eternal kingdom!

John 16:16-22

How can we be prepared—even eager—to see Jesus when He comes again? How does our perspective on life and history, in light of Jesus' second coming, affect our attitudes, our plans, our values, and the diligence with which we work for His cause in His kingdom?

The Messiah
in the
Kingdom of God
His Identity

How is it that you sought Me? Did you not know that I must be in My Father's House?
Luke 2:49

Teaching was an integral part of family life in Jesus' time. The routine of daily living was closely interwoven with the study of Sacred Scripture and the observance of religious laws and rites.

Joseph taught Jesus carpentry; each member of the family contributed to the well-being of the whole. Both parents taught religion—the meaning of the Law and the Prophets, the ritual of recurring festivals, morals and ethical behavior. Passages from the Law, the Psalms, and the Prophets had to be memorized.

Each village had a synagogue where a teacher or "doctor of the law" continued the education of young Hebrew males. At age 6, boys were required to attend the synagogue school. There they were taught Hebrew history and language, the law and its interpretation, and how to understand the meaning of God's Word. The only textbooks were the scrolls of the Scriptures. Reading and writing and memory work were required.

When a boy reached the age of 12, he was considered to be a man. Every man who lived within 15 miles of Jerusalem was obligated to go to the temple to observe the feast of Passover. Many times whole families made the journey. Joseph and Mary accompanied Jesus on His first visit to the temple.

The Passover lasted several days, and when it was over, the families returned to their villages. The women, who traveled more slowly, left in advance of the men. Both groups arranged to meet along the road at a designated area. Therefore we can understand why both Mary and Joseph assumed that Jesus was traveling with the other parent. When they discovered that He was missing, they anxiously returned to Jersualem to look for Him.

Rabbis and their students gathered in the porticos of the temple—the rabbi to expound words of wisdom, the students to ask questions. There were often lively and heated discussions. So it was perfectly natural for Jesus to mingle with such a group. He was the Son of God! Telling His parents that He had to be in His Father's house revealed that truth.

Each one of us needs to ask the same question that Jesus did. Why should I be a part of the learning and worship experience in my Father's house? The reasons seem to be fairly obvious: to increase in wisdom and understanding so that one can not only cope with the stress of 20th-century living but also can be a more effective servant among apathetic people who have little concern for religion or the study of Scripture.

Luke 2:41-51

How would you answer someone who believes that participation in worship, study, and Sacrament is unnecessary?

What did you go out into the wilderness to behold? A reed shaken by the wind? Why then did you go out? To see a man clothed in soft raiment? . . . Why then did you go out? To see a prophet?

Matthew 11:7-9

John the Baptist was in prison; he had dared to confront the mighty Herod, censuring his wickedness. He feared no one. Nothing could quench the fire and zeal of his impassioned preaching. John worshiped a just and holy God—One who would come to judge the world. He had prepared the way for the coming of the Messiah: "He who is mightier than I is coming, the thong of whose sandals I am not worthy to untie" (Luke 3:16). Now in his dungeon, he heard reports about the great crowds who came to hear Jesus and about those who were healed of infirmities. This was not the thundering judge that John had anticipated. Therefore he sent his disciples to Jesus with the question: "Are you He who is to come, or shall we look for another?" In His answer, Jesus implied that the prophecy of Isaiah had been fulfilled—that the Messianic age was here. Those who believed and did not reject Him were blessed indeed.

When John's disciples left Him, Jesus questioned the crowd: "What did you expect to find in the wilderness?" Surely John was not like the tall grasses which grew along the river, buffeted to and fro when the wind blew. He was a man of courage; he never vacillated from the truth. He was not a fine courtier living in a palace; he was an austere man of the desert who dressed in camel's hair and leather. He was a prophet—but more than a prophet! He was the forerunner of

29

Jesus, the Messiah in whom Malachi's prophecy had been fulfilled.

We do not have John the Baptist to point out the Messiah for us, but we have the Savior in His Word of forgiveness and in His sacramental presence. And we have the witness of strong persons down through the ages who refused to compromise their faith in their crucified Savior. William Tyndale was strangled and burned in 1536 for translating the New Testament and parts of the Old into English. But his work survived and was of enduring value.

Matthew 11:2-15; Luke 7:18-28;
Isaiah 29:18-19; 35:5-6; 61:1 ff.; Malachi 3:1

Look around you. Do you see strong persons of faith like John? What motivates them?

Who do men say that the Son of Man is?
Matthew 16:13

Jesus' ministry was coming to a close; the time was at hand to turn toward Jerusalem and Calvary. His disciples had been an intimate part of that ministry, witnesses of His teaching in the simple language of home and field. They had heard compassionate words for those who were healed, the profound eloquence of the parables, the harsh warnings to learned teachers of the law, the moving blessing of little children, the beautiful promises of eternal life, and the constant proclamation of love and forgiveness. They had mingled with the crowds and had heard expressions of wonder and amazement, heartfelt repentance, thanksgiving, and praise. They had experienced hostility and rejection along with Jesus.

"Who do men say that the Son of Man is?" was a poignant query to those closest to Him. Jesus' travels had covered a comparatively small geographic area. The miracles and healings were known to many people by actual witness or by word of mouth. "The blind receive their sight and the lame walk, lepers are cleansed and the deaf hear, and the dead are raised up, and the poor have good news preached to them" (Matthew 11:5). They had seen and heard the Son of Man, but they failed to recognize Him. To many He was John the Baptist or Elijah or Jeremiah or a prophet or a teacher—but not the Christ.

30

That same question has enormous implication for today. Have you not heard it said that Jesus was a revolutionary, a bold and impassioned leader, a teacher of great wisdom, a kind and compassionate physician, a good example to follow? But these are impersonal, empty portrayals. They can be boldly proclaimed without any danger of personal involvement. They demand no allegiance, no commitment, no confession of faith or dependence on Jesus as Savior, no celebration that Jesus is Lord, no understanding of the responsibility of discipleship. They are as heartbreaking today for our living God of grace as they were to Jesus, the Son of Man, 2,000 years ago.

Matthew 16:13-23; Mark 8:27-33

In your everyday associations, what do you learn about Jesus? Is He ever mentioned? How do you testify to His true identity? Why should you?

Who do you say that I am?
Matthew 16:15

Again, Jesus poses a question to His disciples. But it is no longer impersonal; it requires individual response. The collective "they" becomes "you"! It was now necessary for each disciple to look at Jesus in light of everything he had seen and heard and experienced during almost three years of constant fellowship. Each one had shared Jesus' reactions to many diverse and challenging situations—joy and sorrow, stern admonition and gentle counseling, reconciliation and judgment, incomprehensible love and forgiveness, anticipation of danger and future hope. They knew intimately the cost of discipleship. Despair, rejection, loneliness, humiliation, incomprehension, and dissension were shared along with prayer, praise, and thanksgiving. Each one had to search himself, to see himself in relationship to his Master.

Peter saw that Jesus was the promised Messiah, the Christ, the Son of the living God. His insight came as a personal revelation of grace—not from men but from his heavenly Father. This divinely created gift of faith enabled him to see Jesus as his Savior! Peter spoke

31

for himself and for all the disciples. He was an individual within a group confessing his faith in his Savior and Lord. Like Peter, we are truly not alone.

Peter's gift of faith came from God while he stood in the physical presence of Jesus; our gifts of grace come through Word and sacrament as we stand in the glorified presence of Jesus. God revealed His steadfast love for us in the unfolding of the Messianic covenant: first in the call of His chosen people; then through the life, death, and resurrection of His beloved Son; and finally with the gift of the Holy Spirit. The Holy Spirit comes to us in the Gospel and Baptism. He creates faith within us; He helps us to perceive and understand as Peter did; He leads us to repentance; He assures us of our forgiveness over and over again; and He empowers us to be bold confessors as Peter was!

Matthew 16:13-23; Mark 8:27-33

Check your relationship to your Savior. Is He really the Lord of your life as you confess Him to be?

What do you want Me to do for you?
Matthew 20:32

"What do you want Me to do for you?" is a poignant acknowledgment by Jesus of everyone's yearning for God—for something beyond themselves.

Two blind beggars sitting by the side of the road heard a great crowd approaching. Jesus and His disciples along with many other pilgrims were on their way to Jerusalem for the Passover. When they heard that Jesus was passing by, the blind men shouted, "Lord, have mercy on us, Son of David." The people tried to keep them from Jesus, but the beggars refused to be intimidated. They persisted in trying to get Jesus' attention and cried out even more. Jesus stopped and called to them. They came to Him quickly with much anticipation. In response to His question they replied, "Lord, let our eyes be opened." Jesus touched them, and immediately their sight was restored. And they followed Him!

This little story is filled with irony. Two blind beggars "saw" Jesus as the Messiah while the disciples, who could see physically, lacked awareness and understanding of His role. "Son of David" and "Lord" were Messianic titles. For many people at that time these titles had a political connotation, the restoration of the Davidic kingdom. To Jesus the Messiah was the One who came to reconcile all mankind of God.

These two blind beggars surely must have yearned for a life with meaning and peace. To beg is to humiliate oneself. Perhaps because of their circumstance they were more easily able to perceive the mission of the Messiah. They surely were aware of their need for reconciliation. They asked with intense fervor for Jesus' blessing. They ran when He called. When they received forgiveness from their compassionate Savior, they immediately followed Him. In Mark a parallel story about a blind beggar, Bartimaeus, has Jesus saying, "Your faith has made you well."

Jesus' compassion is as real today as it was then. He calls to all who are seeking. He turns no one away. He understands our needs and our yearnings even before we do. He offers forgiveness when we are not aware that we need it. He is concerned about our weakness. He reaches out with inexpressible love to all of His Father's children. His call is the same today, "Come to Me—I will make you whole."

Matthew 20:29-34; Mark 10:46-52

When you look at the lives of those around you, the turmoil in the world, the hopelessness of so many of God's children, what is it that you want from Jesus? Where does it start?

What do you think of the Christ? Whose son is He? . . . How is it that David, inspired by the Spirit, calls Him Lord, saying, "The Lord said to my Lord, sit at My right hand, till I put Thy enemies under Thy feet"? If David calls Him Lord, how is He his son?

Matthew 22:42-45

The Pharisees' conviction that the Messiah was to be a political leader blinded them to Jesus' mission. They dreamed of a kingdom equal in might and splendor to David's and Solomon's, ruled by the

Christ from the lineage of David. He would, therefore, in the dynastic succession, be a son of David.

Jesus refers them to Scripture, Psalm 110:1: "If David calls Him Lord, how is He his son?" The entire Psalm has Messianic implications. Luther called it the chief Psalm of our Lord Jesus Christ. He believed that it alluded to Jesus' divinity, His work, His resurrection and ascension, and His future kingdom. In calling Him Lord, David is saying that the Messiah is greater than he. When he declares that his Lord is sitting "at the right hand of God," he witnesses to the power and authority, the honor and majesty of the Christ who is to carry out the will of His Father. The will of our loving Father is that the Messiah overcome sin, death, and the devil, the great deterrents to the kingdom of God.

Who is the Christ? He is the Lord of David, the Lord of the Pharisees, the Lord of all! He is the Messiah who proclaimed: "Before Abraham was, I am!" Jesus speaks with the authority of the Father; His works are the works of the Father, who dwells in the Son. "I am in the Father and the Father in Me" reveals the immeasurable love of God, who entered history to show us the depth of that love. "I am the Way, and the Truth, and the Life"—Jesus *is* the only way to reconciliation with God; He *is* the only truth revealing God's divine nature and purpose; He *is* the only source of life in God's eternal kingdom. "I am the One who gives you living water"—the water of Baptism which gives new birth. "I am the Good Shepherd"—who gave His life for our salvation. "I am the Resurrection and the Life"— those who believe never die; they walk in newness of life every day. "I am the Bread of Life"—food for the new life. "I am the True Vine"— those who are grafted to Jesus in faith, trust, and obedience to His will are productive disciples in the kingdom of God.

Matthew 22:41-46; Mark 12:35-37; Luke 20:41-44; Psalm 110:1; John 6:35-40; 8:12, 58; 10:11-18; 11:25-26; 14:6-7; 15:1-5; Acts 2:34-38; Hebrews 1:13; 10:12-13

How do you interpret the phrase "sit at My right hand"? How does Jesus' question hint at the two natures of the God-man?

Why do you trouble the woman?
Matthew 26:10

It was several days before the Passover. Jesus, as the Messiah, knew that He would soon be betrayed and turned over to the authorities. The chief priests and elders were already plotting His arrest and crucifixion.

In sharp contrast to the intrigue among the priests and scribes, Jesus and His disciples were reclining together in the home of a friend, enjoying the fellowship of a meal. While they were eating, a woman came to Jesus and in a deeply moving gesture anointed His head with costly perfume. It was a beautiful expression of love and honor—and recognition of Jesus as the Messiah. The expensive ointment was very likely her most precious possession but she gave it gladly in the humility of service.

This lovely gesture was symbolic of the anointing of a king, but One who was soon to die for the sins of humankind. Jesus accepted it as a beautiful gift of love in preparation for His burial. His words were prophetic.

The disciples, however, saw the spontaneous act only as sheer waste—the costly ointment could have been sold for a great deal of money to feed the poor. Mark tells us that it was worth 300 denarii, a year's wages for a laborer.

"Why do you trouble the woman?" tersely reminds the disciples of their spiritual blindness. His constant companions for three years did not understand Jesus' reference to His suffering and death. They did, however, feel Jesus' deep concern for the poor and needy. But, unfortunately, their uneasiness obscured the ethereal beauty and pathos of the woman's love.

We are often guilty of the same spiritual blindness which afflicted Jesus' first disciples. Common sense often dictates lengthy discussion and evaluation of church and personal mission. In the process, the spontaneity of doing a purely lovely thing may be lost. There is place in the kingdom of God for beauty and loveliness as well as practicality. Sharing the fragile beauty of a rose or a spontaneous, loving embrace are as much a part of discipleship as counting and dispensing money.

Unfortunately, we are too often concerned only with appearances, too embarrassed to share our deepest feelings, or even ashamed of displaying affection openly and without reservation. Jesus never was!

Matthew 26:6-13; Mark 14:3-9; John 12:1-8

How do you interpret Jesus' question? What are some of the lovely things that might be shared in the church and in your community?

___

I have shown you many good works from the Father; for which of these do you stone Me? ... Is it not written in your law, 'I said, you are Gods'? If He called them gods to whom the Word of God came ... do you say of Him whom the Father consecrated and sent into the world, 'You are blaspheming,' because I said, I am the Son of God?

John 10:32-36

In the preceding chapters of John there are many instances of Jesus accomplishing mighty works of His Father. John tells us that there were many who believed. But He also tells us that there were many who "sought all the more to kill Him" (John 5:18).

On a wintry day in December Jesus was walking in the Temple on Solomon's porch. It was a place where people came to meditate, and where rabbis came with their students to teach and to argue points of doctrine. It was such a group who accosted Jesus, demanding to know if He was the Christ. Jesus reminded them that "the works which I do in My Father's name . . . bear witness to Me. . . . I and the Father are one." The response of His enemies was to "take up stones again to stone Him." Stoning was the penalty for blasphemy— "because You, being a man, make Yourself God." They were executing judgment without the benefit of a court hearing or without listening to testimony contrary to their obtuse, stubborn mind-set.

Jesus countered their accusations with a question, referring them to Psalm 82:6, where it says of judges: "I say 'You are gods.'" In the opening statement of the Pslam, God had this to say: "How long will you judge unjustly and show partiality to the wicked?" Jesus is reminding His accusers that God had entrusted His Word to them, called them out of slavery to be "sons of the Most High," and that they were now refusing to recognize Him as God's Son. They had made themselves into gods, ignoring the plain evidence of His claims, blindly accusing and judging their Savior.

There are many counterparts to Jesus' accusers today who refuse to see Jesus as Messiah simply because it would drastically interfere with their way of life. Were they to recognize Jesus as Savior and acclaim Him Lord of their lives, it would mean that their jealously guarded pride in position would have to be replaced by servanthood. Their independence from God, which is really dependence on self, would be lost. Self-seeking would have to yield to self-giving. What more could He do to convince anyone of His deity?

John 10:31-39; Psalm 82

How do we stone Jesus? For what reasons do people want to silence Jesus' claims on their lives?

Do you really know Me and know where I am from? (TEV)
John 7:28

It was the time of the Feast of the Tabernacles, the most popular festival of the year. It took place in autumn just after the harvest was finished. The pilgrims who came to Jerusalem to celebrate the feast lived in huts or "tabernacles" made from branches. (The huts are believed to be symbolic of the tents in which the Hebrews lived during their 40-year wandering in the wilderness of Sinai.)

Jesus was in Galilee; He was very reluctant to go to Jerusalem. He had been rejected by His own brothers. He knew that some of His countrymen wanted to kill Him; anything He did would be suspect, open to misinterpretation. Many of these hostile authorities would be in Jerusalem for the feast which would last seven days. So He went privately. But in the middle of the week, He went to the temple to teach. Great crowds came to hear Him.

Jesus' teaching precipitated all kinds of reactions among those who heard Him. Some felt that perhaps He really was the Messiah because the authorities allowed Him to teach openly without interference. But there was a problem. It was commonly believed that the Messiah would appear suddenly, literally out of nowhere, and everyone knew that Jesus came from Nazareth in Galilee! Then there were those who believed that His claim to have come from God was blasphemous.

Jesus answered their misgivings, "Do you really know Me and know where I am from?" Those who had so many doubts and were unable to believe really did not know their God. They could not see that Jesus' physical origin was a part of God's plan. The truth that He was sent by the Father could be grasped only by faith—and for many, their faith was shaky, like a reed blown about by the wind. Some believed because He did signs. Ironically, those who sought to have Him arrested were resisted by the temple police, who refused to have anything to do with him. "No man ever spoke like this man," the police officers reported.

Even today doubters and those with little faith continue to look for signs. Faith, created by the Holy Spirit in Baptism, rooted in the knowledge of God, does not need signs to grow and mature. Doubt itself can be healthy if it leads to dialog, prayer, and meditation, to introspection and awareness of one's inability to "know" Jesus without the resources of Word and sacrament. The only sign we need is the undeniable one of Easter.

John 7:25-52

How do you come to know Jesus? What convinces you of His divine origin?

Where have you laid him? . . . Did I not tell you that if you would believe you would see the glory of God?
John 11:34, 40

Lazarus was dead. When he became ill, Mary and Martha, his sisters, sent word to Jesus that "he whom You love is ill." However, Jesus did not go immediately to Bethany. Instead, He lingered for several days, telling His disciples: "This illness is not unto death; it is for the glory of God, so that the Son of God may be glorified by means of it."

The "glory of God" refers to divine compassion and grace—God's redemptive love for all humankind. It points beyond physical life to eternal life in God's kingdom. But that kingdom already exists for one who believes in Jesus as Savior and Lord. "The kingdom of God comes . . . when our heavenly Father gives us His Holy Spirit, so that by His grace we believe His holy Word and lead a godly life, here

38

in time and hereafter in eternity" (Luther's Small Catechism). Physical death cannot destroy it; it is the pathway to eternal life. This is the truth which Jesus was teaching by Word and sign, but which was so often misunderstood. In everything He did He was revealing the heart of His Father—unfathomable compassion and steadfast love for His beloved humanity.

When Jesus arrived at the home of His friends, Lazarus had been dead for four days. There He found Mary and Martha surrounded by friends and professional mourners, weeping. John tells us that Jesus was moved in spirit, and troubled. He was indignant and almost angry, resentful of the people for their lack of faith and understanding. The mourners exhibited an underlying hypocrisy; supposedly they believed in resurrection, but they mourned as if there were no hope of eternal life at all.

"Could not He who opened the eyes of the blind man have kept this man from dying?" They had missed the point of Jesus' previous signs. This final sign—raising Lazarus from the dead—was to reveal Jesus' power and infinite grace. It revealed the profound love of our incarnate God, who gives life and conquers death, for He came to Judea not only to raise Lazarus from the dead but to face His own death on the cross.

To see only the physical evidence of Jesus' signs is to miss the revelation of God's grace as reconciliation and life-giving love. In each sign that glory of God was revealed—whether it was through changing water to wine, restoring sight, healing illness, straightening crippled limbs, feeding the masses, or raising the dead!

John 11:1-53

Do you see signs of Jesus' power and grace in the world in which you live, in the events of everyday living?

Whom do you seek? . . . Again He asked them, 'Whom do you seek?'
John 18:4, 7

The account of Jesus' last supper with His disciples and His arrest in the Garden is filled with profound theological implications.

During the hours surrounding their last meal together and His farewell discourse, Jesus had tried to prepare the Twelve for their role in discipleship—establishing the Christian church when He would no longer be with them to lead and advise. While they were eating, Jesus identified Judas as the one who would betray Him. Immediately, Judas went out into the darkness of night—and the darkness of evil.

In His deeply moving "high priestly prayer" Jesus not only prayed for Himself but also for His disciples and for the unity of the fledgling church. He knew what He had to face, and He knew that He had to face it alone. Only He could complete the work His Father had given Him. His time had come. "Father, the hour has come; glorify Thy Son that the Son may glorify Thee, since Thou hast given Him power over all flesh, to give eternal life to all whom Thou hast given Him."

After this final, poignant prayer, Jesus led the disciples to the garden on the slope of the Mount of Olives where they had often gathered to pray. Judas knew it well.

When Judas appeared with a band of Roman soldiers and temple police, Jesus went to meet them. He was in command! "Whom do you seek?"—He initiated the interrogation. To their reply, "Jesus of Nazareth," He answered with authority, "I am He." Jesus identified Himself not only as the carpenter from Nazareth but as the Messiah. In what must have been momentary awareness of the power and majesty of the One they had come to arrest, they drew back and fell to the ground. Again Jesus questioned them; again the answer was the same, but with an addition: Jesus requested that His disciples be allowed to leave. Knowing what was ahead of Him, yet thinking only of those whom He came to serve, Jesus' concern was for His friends, who would very soon be battling their own private doubt, insecurity, denial, and the constant threat of temptation and evil.

Jesus fearlessly and positively identified Himself to His accusers. He continues to identify Himself through the work of the Holy Spirit. He gives us confidence and power to be His disciples in the face of hostility, rejection, persecution, and temptation. He freely offers Himself as Advocate, Counselor, and Friend. If this is the One we seek, then we have found Him in the Garden.

John 18:1-9; 17:1 ff

Whom do nonbelievers seek? What are they really looking for? How would Jesus be the answer to their seeking?

Do you say this of your own accord,
or did others say it to you about Me?

John 18:34

Jesus' arrest plunged Him into a maelstrom of events from which there could be no temporal rescue. His enemies were faced with a dilemma. They had charged Jesus with blasphemy: "He has made Himself the Son of God." According to their law, blasphemy was punishable by stoning. But since Rome did not allow them to carry out the death penalty, they took Him to the Roman governor, Pilate, to be tried as an "evildoer." It was absolutely necessary for them to convince Pilate that Jesus was a threat to Rome. The Roman penalty for insurrection was death by crucifixion.

The leaders knew that Jesus was not plotting against Rome—but they saw the overwhelming ovation from the great masses of pilgrims at His entry into Jerusalem as a threat to their hold on the people. Because Jesus had exposed their hypocrisy and apostasy, they felt they had to trick Pilate into sentencing Him to death.

When Jesus was brought to the Praetorium, Pilate asked Him if he was the King of the Jews. Jesus' reply, "Do you say this of your own accord, or did others say it about Me?" is a clarifying question— forcing both a statement of motive and the exposure of monstrous injustice. Jesus calmly stood before Pilate as Examiner and Judge! "Am I a Jew?"—Pilate's cynical reply shows only concern for his precarious political position. Remorse and self-searching for sentencing the Messiah to death would come later. "My kingship is not of this world" affirmed that Jesus was truly the Messiah; He had no political or worldly ambition. Jesus' accusers had outwitted Pilate, who was now caught in a web of his own weakness and fear.

With dignity Jesus testified to His Messianic majesty and glory. He quietly accepted His destiny as our Savior and King. Each of us, drawn to Him by the Spirit, must serve Jesus as Messiah and King of our lives if we are to be disciples. Unlike Pilate, we must resist the temptation to reject Jesus in order to gain approval from worldly peers and powers. Unlike Jesus' enemies, we must resist the temptation to reject Him in order to hold on to the hypocrisy of legalistic, ritualistic, and man-centered religion in which we pretend to appease God with our "good" works, respectability and influence.

How do you know that Jesus is King of kings, Savior of the world, and your own personal Savior?

What is this conversation which you are holding with each other as you walk? . . . What things? . . . Was it not necessary that the Christ should suffer these things and enter into His glory?

Luke 24:17, 19, 26

It was Easter day. Cleopas and a friend were returning from Jerusalem to their home in Emmaus after an earthshaking Passover weekend. They were disciples of Jesus as we are; they were not part of the Eleven. They were deeply saddened by the death of Jesus, bewildered by the turn of events, perplexed by rumors of the empty tomb. The One who they thought was the Christ had come to an untimely end. Their conversation reflected their feelings.

Jesus certainly had not conformed to their idea of the Messiah. He had not defended Himself against charges of blasphemy brought by the Sanhedrin; He showed patience and restraint during His trial by Pilate; He submitted to scourging by the soldiers. Yet He had been in control of those who came to the Garden to arrest Him; with dignity and authority He had interceded for the safety and freedom of the disciples who were with Him. Even on the cross His concern was for others. It was all very strange and disquieting.

When their risen Lord joined them along the way, they did not recognize Him. How sorrowful of heart He must have been at their slowness to believe! In the latter part of His ministry He had tried over and over again to prepare His disciples for His humiliating death—but they did not understand. Nor had He been able to make them understand that He would rise from the dead. Even now Jesus did not give up. Patiently He interpreted the Scriptures to them, showing that it was necessary for Him to suffer before He returned to His Father's kingdom—there to reign with the Father, sharing the glory which was His before the foundation of the world. Resurrection from death to new, glorified life was to be the final act of God's reconciling love. It would open wide the gates to eternal life in His kingdom for all

42

humankind! It would enable His covenant of grace to be carried beyond the confines of Judaism to embrace the whole world.

The glorified Lord returns to His doubting disciples again and again through His Spirit to dispel doubts and uncertainties, to quicken understanding and strengthen faith.

Luke 24:13-27

Do you share your doubts with other Christians? What does Jesus' resurrection mean to you?

Why are you troubled, and why do questionings rise in your hearts? . . . Have you anything here to eat?
Luke 24:38, 41

Jesus' interpretation of the Scriptures failed to move Cleopas and his friend to recognize Him. But they were reluctant to let Him go. Using the excuse that the day was almost gone, Cleopas invited the stranger to stay at his home. Jesus accepted, but contrary to custom, he assumed the role of family head instead of honored guest. (The head of a household always broke bread and offered it to his guests.) When with authority he took the bread and blessed it, broke it and gave it to them, they immediately recognized Him—and Jesus vanished.

Quickly Cleopas and his friend returned to Jerusalem to share their good news with the other disciples. They found the Eleven gathered together in an upper room behind locked doors. There they learned that the glorified Jesus had also appeared to Simon. But they were all still uneasy, unable to grasp the significance of both reports. Suddenly Jesus was in their midst; the risen, glorified Savior was no longer confined to time or space! But the disciples were terribly frightened. They thought He was a ghost, because the doors were locked. "Why do you doubt—why are you troubled? Look at My hands and feet. Touch Me. Give Me something to eat." And He took a piece of fish and ate.

Without the resurrection, the crucifixion would have been entirely meaningless. The resurrection of Jesus from the dead is the foundation of our Christian faith, the authentication of Jesus as the

43

Son of God. Unlike the resurrection of Lazarus, who continued to live like any other human, Jesus' rising from the dead was a transformation into the new life of the new body.

The resurrection is a mystery—beyond the comprehension of our mortal minds. But, grasped by faith, it is the warranty of everlasting life.

Luke 24:28-43

How would you explain resurrection to a young child, a nonbeliever, an agnostic, and a doubter?

Children, have you any fish?

John 21:5

"I'm going fishing"—a simple statement by Peter, charged with confusion and turmoil. He must have felt terribly alone and let down. Three years of intimate fellowship with his Friend and Master were gone; the future was uncertain. Twice Peter had seen his risen Lord— but Jesus had left him as quickly as He had come. There was nothing left to do but to go back home to Galilee and return to fishing.

Thomas, Nathanael, James and John, and two others joined Peter. They fished all night, but they caught nothing. Tired and disappointed, they returned to the shore just as morning was dawning. There on the beach they saw Jesus, but they did not recognize Him. (This was third time that they failed to "see" Jesus.)

Jesus asked them whether they had caught any fish. When they replied that their nets were empty, He commanded them to throw the net over the other side of the boat. Though weary and disheartened, they obeyed. Immediately the net was teeming with fish, almost impossible to haul into the boat. (Here is a remarkable parallel to the miraculous catch of fish when Peter was called to follow Jesus.) The "beloved disciple" then recognized Jesus as the glorified Lord. Impulsive Peter could not wait for the boat to reach the shore.

Jesus had prepared a simple breakfast of bread and fish—but unlike the feeding of the 5,000, where the loaves and fish were provided by a young lad, He provided the meal. As in the Emmaus appearance, the risen Jesus made Himself known to His disciples in association with the breaking of bread.

Jesus calls us from our daily tasks to serve Him in discipleship just as He called Peter and the others from the secular world in which they had tried to escape. He calls us first in Baptism; He sustains us with the bread and wine of His Supper.

The net teeming with fish symbolizes all of humankind throughout the entire world; the unbroken net symbolizes the Kingdom of God, where there is room for everyone—and no one is denied! Our call, like Peter's, is to be fishers of men. Peter's experience is ours, too: When we stray, Jesus seeks us out and calls us back to the only real life—discipleship in His kingdom, where He is the Messiah!

John 21:1-14; Mark 1:16-20; Luke 5:1-11

How many "fish" have you caught? Can you carry out your mission all by yourself? How can you touch the lives of those around you?

The Messiah
in the
Kingdom of God
His Power
and
Authority

Why do you question thus in your hearts? Which is easier, to say to the paralytic, 'Your sins are forgiven,' or to say, 'Rise, take up your pallet and walk'?

Mark 2:8b-9

Jesus was at Capernaum, staying in the home of Peter. His fame had spread throughout Galilee, and wherever He went, crowds of people came to hear Him.

Peter's home was small. Like most of the Palestinian houses, it had only one room, a flat roof, and a staircase going to the roof on the outside. The roof was made of branches or young saplings laid crosswise, fairly close together. The space between the branches was filled with twigs and straw, packed with mud. Traditionally, the door was always open during the day.

Since Peter's home could not accommodate a large group of people, Jesus stood just outside the door to teach. Among those gathered to hear Him were scribes and Pharisees—the teachers of the Law. They had heard of Jesus' unorthodox teaching and His failure to keep their myriad of detailed laws. They were there only to criticize, to oppose, and to judge.

There was a paralytic in the town. When his four friends heard that Jesus was there, they took him on his bed—a cot—to see Jesus. The crowd was so closely packed that they could not get near Him. Consequently, they took the paralytic up on the roof, removed a section of twigs and mud, and lowered the cot to the room below. When Jesus saw their faith, He was moved with compassion and said, "My son, your sins are forgiven."

Immediately the scribes thought to themselves: "Blasphemy! Who can forgive sins but God alone?" Their blindness prevented them from "seeing" Jesus, the Son of God.

Jesus, aware of their misgivings, asked them, "Why do you question in your hearts? Which is easier, to say, 'Your sins are forgiven' or 'Rise and walk'?" To convince them that He has the authority to forgive sins, He asked the paralytic to pick up his cot and walk. The man obeyed—to the amazement of those who saw and heard.

Now, if the Incarnation is the ultimate revelation of God's grace—God coming to His children, freely giving of Himself, to seek out and reconcile sinners to God, then this is indeed the One who can forgive sins.

Mark 2:1-12; Matthew 9:1-8; Luke 5:17-26

How do you apply "Forgive us our sins as we forgive those who sin against us"?

Do you see anything?
Mark 8:23-24

Jesus and His disciples came to the town of Bethsaida. There some townspeople brought to Jesus a man who was blind. They begged Him to heal the man.

Blindness was a very common tragedy in the Middle East; it still is today. Disease of the eye was usually due to poor hygiene and the lack of good sanitation practices and facilities. Scarring of the eye often resulted in blindness.

Jesus took the blind man out of the town, where they could be alone. There he "spit on his eyes and laid his hands upon him." (In ancient times saliva was believed to have healing effects. Therefore the man who was blind could readily understand Jesus' seemingly unorthodox method of healing.) The man had obviously not been blind from birth. When Jesus asked him, "Do you see anything?" the man replied, "I see men; but they look like trees, walking." Jesus again laid His hands on the man's eyes—and he saw everything clearly. What happened was a miracle—a demonstration of the power of Jesus, the Messiah. Even though the healing was not instantaneous but in two stages, it was a miraculous cure. But it was a healing done privately; Jesus sent the man who could now see to his home, telling him not to "even enter the village."

Jesus' power was not limited to the healing of physical blindness; it also touched the spiritual blindness of His disciples. He gradually opened their blind, obtuse eyes to the truth that He was the Messiah—that His power and authority were from God and that God sent Him to bring forgiveness and reconciliation to all His children. "I and the Father are one" (John 10:30).

We are often as blind and obtuse as were those early disciples. God continues to stoop down to us, seeking us out, helping us to understand—through the power of His Holy Spirit. Sometimes our response to His grace is slow and gradual like the healing of the blind man. Sometimes our growth in grace—faith, trust, understanding, and wisdom—increases steadily but rapidly at an ever-increasing pace. Sometimes there are spectacular, instant conversion experiences. But each response is the work of God!

We live in the age of the Spirit! We are not cautioned to tell no one. Instead, we are commanded to "Go and tell"—to share the Gospel of God's steadfast, unending love with all people!

Mark 8:22-26

What does God expect us to see?—with our physical sight?—with our spiritual sight?

Why are you afraid? Have you no faith?
Mark 4:40

The Sea of Galilee is very small compared to the vast oceans of the world—only about 13 miles long and 8 miles wide. Most of the time it looks calm and tranquil, but it is extremely capricious. Violent windstorms appear suddenly, without warning, churning the sea into huge waves and blinding spray.

Jesus and His disciples were in a boat crossing the Sea of Galilee. Jesus was asleep, trusting implicitly in His Father's power to care for Him. Suddenly the winds came with a fury, whipping up the sea and almost swamping the boat. The disciples were terrified. They wakened Jesus and cried out to Him to save them. With authority He rebuked the winds and the waves—and the sea became calm. The men were amazed at His power.

This miracle must have had deep meaning for the disciples, familiar as they were with the Old Testament. It speaks of the power of God being demonstrated in the ability to control the wind and the sea (Psalm 46:1-2; 93:3-4). Storm was the metaphor for evil forces (Psalm 69:1-2). One's capacity to sleep peacefully indicated perfect trust and faith in God's power to protect and sustain (Job 11:18-19; Proverbs 3:23-24).

"Why are you afraid? Have you no faith?" Jesus was always teaching—preparing His disciples for their role in the church that was to be. Here He was teaching by example, showing His absolute trust in

His Father. God never sleeps—He watches over His loved ones through calm and calamity. He is always in control!

The relative calm of discipleship today can be shattered without warning by the storms of fear, doubt, emotional upheaval, illness, or misunderstanding. Like those in the boat, our faith and trust may be buffeted about, even weakened. By ourselves we are helpless. At such times we need to remember Jesus' power and authority, and demonstrate by our trust that He is the Ruler of the universe, who will guide and protect both us and His church.

Mark 4:35-41; Matthew 8:23-27; Luke 8:22-25

Have there been times in your life when panic or weak faith prevented you from relying on God's grace?

What is your name?

Mark 5:9

It was late in the evening; Jesus had stilled the storm on the Sea of Galilee. With His disciples He landed on the eastern shore, fairly close to the village of the Gerasenes, a predominately Gentile community. The area was extremely desolate, with many tombs among the caves which dotted the hillside. It was not a pleasant place during the day, and it probably was positively frightening when night fell.

When Jesus got out of the boat, a man with an unclean spirit came out of the tombs. He was unable to live anywhere else; everyone in the nearby village was terrified of him. He continually screamed; he was insensitive to pain, often injuring himself on the rocks by his demented thrashing. He had abnormal strength; no chains could bind him. The evil spirits were very real to this poor, tortured man.

The spirits recognized the divinity of Jesus. They knew Jesus' overwhelming power over them. The man ran to Jesus and "worshiped Him, saying: 'What have You to do with me, Jesus, Son of the Most High God?'" Jesus immediately commanded the evil spirits to leave the man. Jesus asked the spirits: "What is your name?" "My name is Legion" testified to the formidable multitude of demons who had possessed the man. The demons left the man and entered a herd of swine nearby. The swine swiftly rushed headlong into the sea.

The herdsmen fled in terror to the village to tell what had happened. The people who came to see were just as frightened; they requested Jesus to leave their country. No natural power, no human being, had ever been able to help the unfortunate man. In ancient times people were afraid of and in awe of those with apparent supernatural power—the shaman, the medicine man, the exorcist, the faith healer.

The man who had been healed by Jesus begged to go along with Him, but Jesus refused. His insistence that the man remain among his Gentile family and community would be continual convincing evidence of Jesus' divinity, His power and authority—an early indication that His Gospel was to go beyond Judaism.

"What is your name?" our Lord asks the demons that plague us today. Pride, lust for power and dominion over the lives of others, dissipation, addiction, false witness and slander, chaos in society—God has authority over all these perversions! He liberates all those who, in faith and denial of self, accept His compassionate offer of harmony with Himself and the responsibility He gives them to share that compassion with their fellow persons in family, community, nation, and world.

Mark 5:1-20

What "demons" affect your life? How does faith in Christ disperse them?

Do you believe that I am able to do this?
Matthew 9:28

Two blind men followed Jesus into the home in which He was staying. "Have mercy on us, Son of David" they pleaded. Mercy refers to God's love for all humankind, His steadfast love and compassion for those who suffer and are alienated from God. The moving cry of the blind men revealed that they "saw" Jesus as the Messiah who could save them.

"Do you believe that I am able to do this?" Jesus asked for a confession of faith from each of the men. They were alone with Him, away from the noise and confusion of the crowds. There was no one there to prompt them. Each one answered, "Yes, Lord." Jesus touched their eyes, and immediately they could see. Their faith in Jesus' healing love had made them whole.

Matthew tells us that Jesus warned them not to tell anyone about their healing. He did not want to be known only as a miracle worker. His work was to offer forgiveness and reconciliation to all persons— the sick and the healthy, the crippled and the whole, the blind and those who see, the deaf and those who hear. The peace of forgiveness is the great healing that Jesus today bestows freely on each of us who believe in Him.

There are those in our day who insist that if one prays for healing and if one's faith is strong enough, Jesus will heal any infirmity. Somehow this belittles the wisdom of our Lord. It presumes to know the mind of God, to elevate humankind to equality with Him. It fails to "see" that God's primary will and purpose in sending His beloved Son to suffer and die was to reconcile, to bring back into harmony with Himself, all of His suffering children. The "peace which passes all understanding" is the most precious gift one can receive. It brings spiritual sight—the awareness of the infinite depth of God's love and compassion.

Matthew 9:27-31

In what ways are faith and healing related?

Have you not read what David did, when he was hungry, and those who were with him: how he entered the house of God and ate the bread of the presence, which it was not lawful for him to eat nor for those who were with him, but only for the priests? Or have you not read in the law how on the sabbath the priests in the temple profane the sabbath, and are guiltless?

Matthew 12:3-5

Jesus and His disciples went through a grain field on the sabbath. The fields were planted in long rows; the spaces between them were common walkways often used by travelers. Because they were hungry, Jesus and His disciples picked some grain, husked the kernels, and ate them. Immediately they were confronted by the legalistic Pharisees who accused them of breaking the sabbath law.

The Pharisees and scribes adhered to strict laws with innumerable ramifications and interpretations. On the sabbath one was not to light a fire, prepare a meal, draw water, go on a journey, kill an animal, reap a crop, thresh grain, or carry a burden. A burden was defined as anything which weighed more than two dried figs. The law allowed a hungry traveler to hand-pick grain from a neighbor's field, but if he used a sickle he broke the law. The law allowed him to go into a neighbor's vineyard, pick grapes, and eat them, but if he put them into a jar he broke the law. The law was an intolerable burden, impossible to keep. Rules had replaced concern for humanity.

To the legalistic mind of the Pharisee, picking the grain was reaping; husking it by rubbing it between the fingertips was threshing. That was the essence of their charge that Jesus was breaking the law. They were using their petty laws to renounce the Son of God.

Jesus refuted them with a powerful argument from the Scriptures. When David was fleeing from the wrath of Saul, he came to Nob, to the priest Ahimelech, asking for bread. The only bread available was the bread of the Presence, which was kept in the Holy Place of the sanctuary. It was a reminder of God's covenant with Israel, His goodness and mercy. Each sabbath fresh loaves were placed in the Holy Place. The old loaves were to be eaten only by the priests in the sanctuary. This was the bread that Ahimelech gave to David. Literally, the priest was breaking the law—he gave "holy" bread to David.

Jesus abhorred legalism and ritualism which denied mercy and love. In His ministry compassion always took precedence over ritual. "Love is the fulfilling of the Law." By practicing and preaching love, Jesus was fulfilling the will of God.

Matthew 12:1-8; Luke 6:1-5; 1 Samuel 21:1-6

Have you seen legalism taking precedence over mercy in the religious practices of our day? How? What can be done about it?

What man of you, if he has one sheep and it falls into a pit on the sabbath, will not lay hold of it and lift it out?

Matthew 12:11

Jesus went into a synagogue and there He saw a man with a withered hand. But Jesus saw not only a person with a crippled hand—He saw a person who was reduced to the indignity of begging, a man without self-respect or hope because of a disability. In compassion, Jesus healed him.

There were Pharisees present in the synagogue, constantly listening and observing Jesus in an attempt to trap Him, to discredit Him to the authorities. When they asked Jesus, "Is it lawful to heal on the sabbath?" He replied with a counter-question, a common method of dialog among rabbis.

The Pharisees had replaced God's law with innumerable laws of their own. According to their laws, healing could be done on the sabbath only to save life. Any other healing had to wait until the day after the Sabbath. It was lawful to "do good"—to comfort mourners, to visit the sick, and to pray. The law also said that if a sheep fell into a pit, his owner could carry food and water to it.

With his question and answer, Jesus rebuked the Pharisees for their stubborn insistence on following insensitive, destructive rules, thereby ignoring the well-being of one of God's children. "It is lawful to do good on the sabbath!" With that, Jesus healed the man's withered hand, deliberately breaking the Sabbath law forbidding "work."

Jesus may have ignored the traditions of the elders, but He was faithful to the intent of the Ten Commandments: "You shall love the Lord your God with all your heart, and with all your soul, and with all your mind. This is the great and first commandment. And a second is like it, You shall love your neighbor as yourself" (Matthew 22:37-39). In their attempt to carry out their own rules, the Pharisees denied the spirit of God's law. Jesus came to show the heart of the Father in everything He did. Thereby He fulfilled the Law! Not to do good on the sabbath is to do evil. The healing of forgiveness cannot wait until the following day; restoring a person to spiritual wholeness can never wait.

The apostle Paul, who had been the Pharisee Saul, denounced those who observed "the form of religion but denied the power of it" (2 Timothy 3:5)—people who go through the motions of worship but fail to see the intent of the Law: the exercise of perfect love.

Do you see the metaphor of the Good Shepherd in Jesus' question? How does it relate to forgiveness?

Every kingdom divided against itself is laid waste, and no city or house divided against itself will stand; and if Satan casts out Satan, he is divided against himself; how then will his kingdom stand? And if I cast out demons by Beelzebul, by whom do your sons cast them out? . . . Or how can one enter a strong man's house and plunder his goods, unless he first binds the strong man?

Matthew 12:25-27, 29

The name "Beelzebul" was an ancient title for a god; in Canaan he was known as the lord of the temple, the lord of the house, or the lord of the flies. In Jewish literature pagan deities were often identified with evil spirits; Beelzebul was the enemy, the prince of demons, Satan—but not a god.

Jesus' exorcism of a blind and dumb demoniac caused consternation and confusion among the crowds who witnessed the healing. The Pharisees, seizing upon the bewilderment of the people, accused Jesus of casting out demons by the power of Satan—a not very subtle maneuver to discredit Jesus further. But again, Jesus discredited them, even to passing extreme judgment on their bold hypocrisy when He said: "Blasphemy against the Spirit will not be forgiven."

Jesus' question is an indictment of the Pharisees for inciting division among the people. Israel should have been the house of God, but the leaders continually caused turmoil among those whom they were to serve. The Pharisees blasphemed because they called God's work Satan's work! Furthermore, there were also exorcists among the Judaists—but these were supposedly not doing Satan's work.

Division within any family, community, kingdom, or nation is destructive. Jesus' power "by the Spirit of God" revealed that the new Messianic kingdom had actually broken into the world. His work was to save God's children from sin and the power of Satan. Jesus is the enemy of Satan, of all the evil forces that seek to destroy humankind's relationship with God. Jesus is the One who could enter the strong man's house to overcome him and stop his evil work—God Himself acting through His Son. The crucial victory over Satan took place on Calvary when the "Seed of the woman" (Jesus) crushed the serpent's (Satan's) head.

There is a lesson here for each of us—we cannot ignore its implications: "He who is not with Me is against Me, and he who does not gather with Me scatters."

Matthew 12:22-32; Luke 11:14-23

What indications of the disruptive forces of evil do you see in the "house of God" and in your community?

How many loaves have you?
Matthew 15:34

"How many loaves have you?" Those words haunt us—that question will not give us peace. Why? Because the gaunt faces of hungry children covered with flies, looking out of hopeless eyes, will not leave us alone. Some eyes are still filled with pain and yearning, others are dull and lifeless, the spark of hope almost burned out. Television brings suffering in India, Southeast Asia, Indonesia, Africa, and South America right into our homes. We must not allow the instant and repetitive coverage by newspersons to numb our minds and souls so that we become insensitive to the horrible starvation on our planet!

Jesus had been teaching and healing people throughout Galilee. Now He went on from Tyre and Sidon and passed along the Sea of Galilee. Great crowds followed Him, bringing "the lame, the maimed, the blind, the dumb, and many others," and Jesus healed them. Many of them, impressed by the healing, were beginning to believe; at least, "they glorified the God of Israel."

Jesus had deep compassion for the people; they had not eaten good, sustaining food for three days. He was reluctant to send them home "lest they faint on the way." The compassion Jesus felt was not some sentimental, emotional pity. It was the compassion of our Savior, who agonized over lost souls, who loved them with inexpres-

57

sible love, who would willingly die to save them. The final Passover was soon to come. So, with seven loaves of bread and a few bits of fish, Jesus fed 4,000 people.

The pilgrims in the wilderness had a foretaste of the feast to come. The Bread of life—which is the way our Savior refers to Himself in John 6—brings forgiveness of sins, life, and salvation. But the new life that Jesus gave us is meaningless if we do not accept the responsibility of discipleship. Miracles today can occur through the work of a faithful, caring church—people with the compassionate heart of Christ sharing the abundance of their resources with those who are starving.

"Gather up the fragments left over, that nothing may be lost" implies more than just the sharing of God's bounty; it condemns all the waste and misuse of the resources of our planet, which are the creative work of God. If we truly love God, we will cease to be a nation of gluttons, spoilers, and materialists.

Matthew 15:32-39; Mark 8:1-10; John 6:1-14, 35

How can we carry out Jesus' command to feed the hungry, refresh the thirsty, and care for the ill?

O faithless and perverse generation, how long am I to be with you? How long am I to bear with you?

Matthew 17:17

Jesus came down from the mountaintop experience of His transfiguration to be confronted by a group of disciples who had exhibited a surprising amount of weak faith. He came back to confusion, anxiety, and doubt—the reality of the weakness of those who were to do greater works than He would accomplish in His lifetime. Those works include taking His Gospel of reconciliation, forgiveness, and hope to all the nations of the world after He returned to the Father. Were He in our midst today, He would find that there is no change despite the fact that we have the benefit of His indwelling Spirit to push us, to catch us when we stumble, to strengthen faith, and to encourage us.

A distraught father had brought his epileptic son to some of

Jesus' disciples to be healed, but they failed. We do not know which disciples these were, whether they were among the Twelve or the other (unnamed) disciples who also followed Jesus. We do know that Peter, James, and John were on the mountain with Jesus, witnesses to His transfiguration.

Jesus did what the disciples were unable to do; He drove out the demon from the boy at the request of the boy's father. The boy asked nothing of Jesus, but in His compassion for the spiritual well-being of the boy, Jesus healed him. Jesus was and is God! He had the power and the authority to rebuke the evil spirit, to save the boy.

The disciples were frustrated by their failure to heal the boy; the father was critical of the disciples' inability to heal his son. They were unable to function with dignity and calm; neither were they able to reflect confidence in their Messiah.

Our "healing" responsibility is the same as that of those early disciples—to share boldly our experience of God's grace and redemptive power. But we do fail. Self-pride, the fear of criticism and derision, doubt about our ability to speak with conviction, social stratificatizn, the specter of failure—these are the destructive forces which hinder faith. We are sinners and failures but, at the same time, also saints and achievers—forgiven and empowered to try again and again to follow Jesus' example of service and sacrifice.

Matthew 17:14-20; Mark 9:14-29; Luke 9:37-43

Can you think of times when you have succeeded and times when you have failed? What made the difference?

The baptism of John, whence was it?
From heaven or from men?
Matthew 21:25

It was the last week of Jesus' earthly life. He had entered the city of Jerusalem, acclaimed by great crowds of people who had come to celebrate the Passover. He had "cleansed the temple" to the consternation of His enemies. Now, several days later, Jesus had come to the temple to teach; He was still popular with the masses of pilgrims. There He was accosted by the chief priests and elders, members of the Sanhedrin. Trying to discredit Him in front of the people they asked: "By what authority are You doing these things?"

"These things" referred to the cleansing of the temple—driving out the merchants and the money changers, teaching and healing. The chief priests believed themselves to be the final authority in all temple matters; only rarely did even Rome interfere. But, as usual, they were blind to the message of the Son of God. They missed the profound theological significance of Jesus' actions.

Jesus replied to the chief priests' question with a counter-question: "The baptism of John, whence was it? From heaven or from men?" The priests were in a predicament. They could not deny that John was a prophet; that might precipitate rebellion among the pilgrims to whom John was a hero, a messenger sent from God. If they admitted that John's authority came from God, Jesus could very well ask why they then refused to believe in Him. (The Jews recognized the office of prophet to be second only to the Messiah, who was also a prophet.) The chief priests refused to answer, and so did Jesus. He had rejected their authority to question Him! His was the supreme authority; He was the Messiah, God's Son.

Matthew 21:23-27; Mark 11:27-33

What do you see as the function of the church? What are Christ's credentials for His governing of His church?

Have I been with you so long, and yet you do not know Me, Philip? He who has seen Me has seen the Father; how can you say, "Show us the Father"? Do you not believe that I am in the Father and the Father in Me?

John 14:9-10

Jesus and His disciples—except for Judas—were gathered in an upper room in Jerusalem. They had experienced the fellowship, the communion, of their last supper together. It was a difficult time for Jesus; He knew He would soon be leaving them. He had tried in many ways to prepare the disciples for the cataclysmic events that would accompany His departure and for their eventual arduous role in establishing the church. He had revealed the Father's heart: "If you had known Me, you would have known My Father also; henceforth you know Him and have seen Him." Jesus, true God, had healed the sick, fed the hungry, given strength to the oppressed, hope to the exploited, and had taught by word and example God's purpose and will for all His creatures.

The Greeks and the Jews to whom John was writing believed that God was invisible, that no one had ever seen God or would ever see Him. The Torah said that no one could see God and live. So it was rash of Philip to say: "Lord, show us the Father, and we shall be satisfied." Jesus answered in what must have been deep sadness: "How could you not know Me after all this time? Do you not understand that the words I have shared with you are the words of the Father who dwells in Me? At least believe Me for the sake of the works I have done."

The works—the words and the deeds—of our incarnate God are the basis for our faith. We do not believe because we see with our eyes. Like Philip we, too, have been shown the heart of the Father. The Spirit of God, working through His Word and sacraments, has revealed God to us. But we do not always believe implicitly, and we, too, often ask for material proof to ease our doubts. We are fortunate beyond description that God who lived as man, Jesus, understands our doubts and spiritual frailties and that He is always present to persuade and recommission us to do His work.

That work is boldly to share our faith in our living God who loved us so much that He sent His only Son to die for the sins of all humankind—by recounting the compassionate, loving deeds and self-sacrifice of Jesus. Then we are revealing the loving face of the Father. "I do not pray for these only, but also for those who believe in Me through their word, that they may all be one; even as Thou, Father, art in Me, and I in Thee . . . so that the world may believe that Thou hast sent Me" (John 17:20-21).

John 14:1-14

How do you bear witness to the works of God? to the truth that Jesus and the Father are one?

The Messiah
in the
Kingdom of God
His Mission

How are we to buy bread,
so that these people may eat?

John 6:5

It was at the end of Jesus' Galilean ministry. With His disciples Jesus crossed the north end of the Sea of Galilee by boat and went into the hills. Later, "lifting up His eyes," He saw a great crowd of people coming to Him. They had crossed the Jordan River at the ford of Bethsaida, just north of the sea—a long and dusty walk. Turning to Philip, Jesus asked him how they could buy bread to feed these people. It seemed to be a perfectly logical question since Philip's home was in Bethsaida; he would know what was available in the village. Philip's answer was very human—it was impossible to buy bread for such a crowd even if they had a lot of money. Jesus, of course, knew what He was going to do. There was no human solution to the problem; what was impossible for humankind was possible for God. Philip's eyes were still blind to the power and spiritual mission of the Master he followed.

It was the time of the feast of Passover, one of three which Jesus celebrated during His ministry. It was not the final one. Aside from the overwhelming physical miracle, there was profound symbolism in the feeding of the 5,000. To the Jews it would recall a similar event during the time of Moses when God fed His chosen people with manna. Their words, "This is indeed the prophet who is to come into the world!" are reminiscent of the words of Moses, "The Lord your God will raise up for you a prophet like me from among you" (Deuteronomy 18:15).

To Jesus the Passover would be the time when He would obediently be the sacrifice to reconcile the human race to God. "I am the Bread of Life. Your fathers ate the manna in the wilderness, and they died. This is the bread which comes down from heaven, that a man may eat of it and not die. I am the Living Bread which comes down from heaven; if anyone eats of this bread, he will live forever; and the bread which I shall give for the life of the world is My flesh."

Jesus came to save everyone—He wants no one lost. He offered Himself, a legacy of eternal life—forgiveness of sin which bestows life and salvation. He offers spiritual food to make us one with those who have gone before, with those who call upon His name today throughout the world, and with those who are yet to come.

The bread we share—rice, flour, and other foods—satisfies only the physical needs of some of the world's poor and hungry. It cannot prevent death. "The Living Bread which comes down from heaven" satisfies the spiritual needs of all humanity.

John 6:1-51

How can we "buy bread" in order to share the Living Bread of heaven with the spiritually starving?

Do you take offense at this? Then what if you were to see the Son of Man ascending where He was before?

John 6:61-62

On the day after Jesus had fed the multitude, the people got into boats and crossed the Sea of Galilee seeking Him. When they reached Him, they were confronted with Jesus' matter-of-fact statement: "You seek Me, not because you saw signs, but because you ate your fill of the loaves. Do not labor for the food which perishes, but for the food which endures to eternal life, which the Son of Man will give to you." He then followed with a powerful proclamation: "I am the Bread of Life." The Jews, including some of Jesus' followers, were offended by His allusion to eating His flesh and drinking His blood—a hint of the Lord's Supper which was yet to come.

Jesus was both God and man. As man He came to earth to do the will, the work of the Father—to bring back into harmony with God all of His children who were drifting in a sea of doubt, apprehension, weak faith, despair, and unbelief. Just as bread sustains physical life, so the spiritual bread which comes as a result of Jesus' self-sacrifice sustains the God-creature relationship of reconciliation.

There were three groups of people involved in this episode: the crowd of people, many of Jesus' disciples who were not part of the Twelve, and the Twelve who were His constant companions. Many of the disciples were disquieted by Jesus' reference to flesh and blood. They found it unpleasant and unacceptable. They took the words of Jesus in a crassly literal way. Consequently they rejected their Savior. They failed to comprehend His mission.

Ah, but if He was one who came down from heaven like manna

and was indeed going to ascend to heaven—then He might be the food they needed and should have been seeking as much as the loaves and fishes. If it was a king they were looking for to feed them forever, then here He was and would be forever—a King on His ascended throne.

John 6:35-65

How would your knowledge of the death, resurrection, and ascension of Jesus make it easier to accept His words in this text than it was for the pre-Calvary crowd?

What do you think? If a man has a hundred sheep, and one of them has gone astray, does he not leave the ninety-nine on the mountains and go in search of the one that went astray?

Matthew 18:12

Just before speaking this beautiful parable, Jesus refers to the "little ones." "Little ones" means not simply children but those pilgrims young in faith who may not understand the extent and power of God's grace, who do not yet perceive their Savior with deep assurance, who may easily fall into rebellion and sin, and who may become self-righteous from lack of teaching and guidance. When Jesus admonished each disciple and teacher to "humble" himself like a child, He used "child" as a symbol of the humility which allows God to be God, which trusts implicitly in His love, and which is obedient to His will. It is the humility which acknowledges one's need of a Savior. It is the humility which depends on God's grace to accomplish one's mission. It is the humility of worship, prayer, thanksgiving, fellowship, and servanthood. These are the selfless concern of the Good Shepherd. "So it is not the will of My Father who is in heaven that one of these little ones should perish."

In Palestine the pastures were in hill country with many gullies and ravines. There were not vast areas of flat pastures or high mountain meadows such as we are accustomed to in our country. So it was easy for sheep to stray and get lost and to move quickly out of the shepherd's sight.

In His parable and question Jesus is revelaing the heart of the Good Shepherd, who is always seeking the lost and those who stray. We, too, are to be seeking shepherds, each one responsible for the spiritual and temporal well-being of every person in our congregation and on our planet. We are to nurture and encourage those with young faith; we are to support them if they find the going too hard. We can do this because in Baptism we are called by name; we are renewed and sustained in the Lord's Supper; we are empowered by the Holy Spirit.

Perhaps we may feel that our mission to all of God's little ones is too awesome a task. If we do, we can take heart that we have a Shepherd who is always looking after us, and guardian angels who watch over us.

Matthew 18:1-4, 10-14; Luke 15:3-7

How can you leave the security of the ninety-nine (the church) to search for the one who went astray? Will he or she be outside of the church?

Have you never read in the Scriptures: 'The very stone which the builders rejected has become the head of the corner; this was the Lord's doing, and it is marvelous in our eyes'?

Matthew 21:42

In both the Old and New Testaments, "cornerstone" is a figure of speech with Messianic overtones. Literally, it can either be the cornerstone or the keystone in construction. Figuratively, it means to support, uphold, buoy up, sustain, or nurture.

The cornerstone of a building is the first stone laid; it determines the direction of the walls and the stability of the structure. Without a strong and true cornerstone, the building would be in jeopardy; it is the fundamental element for permanence or survival. The keystone is the uppermost stone and the last one set into an arch, which holds all the parts together; without it, the entire structure would collapse.

Jesus' question to the chief priests and elders was a denunciation of their rejection of His Messiahship. He used their own Scripture to condemn them; His question repeats Psalm 118:22-23. Isaiah (28:16 f.)

67

prefigured the Messiah in these words:
Therefore thus says the Lord God,
"Behold, I am laying in Zion for a foundation
a stone, a tested stone,
And I will make justice the line,
and righteousness the plummet."
God said that His kingdom was to be a living temple, not made with hands, not like the temple in Jerusalem, but a temple whose cornerstone would be Jesus, whose plumbline would be justice and righteousness, whose building stones would be those in whom God's Spirit dwells.

Jesus' question was followed with judgment: "Therefore I tell you, the kingdom of God will be taken away from you and given to a nation producing the fruits of it." That "nation" was the Christian church, whose cornerstone is Jesus.

Christ, Thou art the sure Foundation,
Thou the Head and Cornerstone;
Chosen of the Lord and precious,
Binding all the Church in one;
Thou Thy Zion's Help forever
And her Confidence alone.   *(The Lutheran Hymnal, 466:1)*

Matthew 21:33-46; Mark 12:1-12; Luke 20:9-18

How do we show by our lives that our faith is built on Christ as the cornerstone?

Elijah does come first to restore all things; and how is it written of the Son of Man, that He should suffer many things and be treated with contempt?

Mark 9:12

Elijah was a fearless prophet during the reign of King Ahab in the mid-800s B. C. His fervor and zeal were directed twoard removing all remnants of pagan cults which had perverted the religion of the Israelites. They had turned away from God—they worshiped the pagan god Baal, they no longer loved mercy and kindness, nor did they do justice or walk humbly with their God. Elijah forcefully preached repentance!

In accordance with Malachi 4:5 it was expected that Elijah would herald the coming of the Messiah. He was conceived to be a powerful figure who would purify the temple cult and the priesthood before the Messiah would come. He would restore peace and harmony; he would settle controversies; he would correct social injustice.

Elijah appeared as a representative of the prophets when Jesus was transfigured. Peter, James, and John were part of that mysterious event. They saw Jesus speak with Elijah and Moses; they heard God's voice from a cloud: "This is My beloved Son; listen to Him."

The disciples were filled with awe and wonder at the dazzling vision they had seen. God Himself had identified Jesus as His Son, the Messiah—yet the scribes insisted that Elijah had to come before the Messiah appeared. It was all very confusing.

Jesus assured them that Elijah had, indeed, come first. The prediction that Elijah was to precede the advent of the Messiah was fulfilled in the ministry of John the Baptist. "'I tell you that Elijah has already come, and they did not know him, but did to him whatever they pleased. So also the Son of Man will suffer at their hands.' Then the disciples understood that He was speaking to them of John the Baptist" (Matthew 17:12-13).

Elijah, John the Baptist, and Jesus came with the same message of repentance and redemption. They were all treated with scorn and contempt. They were all rejected by the authorities and many of the people. John and Jesus were horribly put to death.

But the lesson of the Transfiguration is the same for us today as it was for Peter, James, and John—the suffering and humiliation of the cross is necessary, but it is transcended by the glory and peace of the Resurrection.

Mark 9:2-13; Matthew 17:1-13

What is the cost of proclaiming the redemption of Christ in our world today? In your life?

Are there not twelve hours in the day?
John 11:9

Jesus never turned aside from His mission; He never wasted any of His precious time; He never procrastinated. In every event of His life, He was the initiator; He was in control. His will was to do God's work—to accomplish God's purpose and will in the redemption of all humankind. His time was now short; there was no waiting to finish His task. Therefore when His disciples were fearfully reluctant to return to Judea because the authorities were "seeking to stone Him," Jesus replied: "Are there not twelve hours in the day? If anyone walks in the day, he does not stumble, because he sees the light of this world. But if anyone walks in the night, he stumbles, because the light is not in him."

The Jewish day was divided into 12 equal hours; it began at sunrise and ended abruptly at sunset. It was just about impossible to finish the work of the daytime after night fell. Those who lived in mud-brick homes had only the light from a dimly flickering oil lamp. It was difficult to travel by night; there were many pitfalls along the way—hedgerows of thorny shrubs, low rock walls, potholes in the roadway, stones and boulders.

In the New Testament "stumble" means to fall into a pit or trap which can cause one to sin, to follow evil, to walk apart from the light of God's love, or to offend another by leading him out of light into darkness.

"He who says he is in the light and hates his brother is in the darkness still. He who loves his brother abides in the light, and in it there is no cause for stumbling. But he who hates his brother is in the darkness and walks in the darkness, and does not know where he is going, because the darkness has blinded his eyes."

(1 John 2:9-11)

Jesus is the Light we live by while it is still day. He is the Light that seeks out every sinner, guiding him away from the enticement of temptation, forgiving him when he stumbles. To walk in the light is to love God and our fellow persons, to be a loving, caring witness to that light.

Jesus gave His life to protect us from the night of darkness. Living in darkness results in hatred, bitterness, dissatisfaction, resentment, fear, dissension, and disregard for the suffering of others. We avoid darkness when we courageously proclaim in word and deed our love for our living God and His beloved children. None of us knows how much time we have left to do God's work; we must work with a profound sense of urgency!

John 11:7-10; Luke 13:33; John 9:4; 12:35

How can we use our days wisely in service and commitment to God's work?

I am the Resurrection and the Life; he who believes in Me, though he die, yet shall he live, and whoever lives and believes in Me shall never die. Do you believe this?

John 11:25-26

Martha had tremendous faith. She recognized Jesus' power: "I know that whatever You ask from God, God will give You." She firmly believed that Jesus could have healed Lazarus. She also believed in the resurrection of the dead which would come at the last day, the end of time as we know it. This is the same Martha whom Jesus had reproved for criticizing her quiet, listening sister.

It is so easy for us to look back and see the weaknesses of Jesus' disciples that somehow we fail to see the strength of their faith. Martha's faith had matured—and now Jesus answered her faith in Him with the ultimate proclamation of His ministry; "I am the Resurrection and the Life; he who believes in Me, though he die, yet shall he live, and whoever lives and believes in Me shall never die. Do you believe this?"

Martha's faith was not really demonstrated in the account of Jesus' earlier visit. But now, in her bereavement, she gave a strong witness of her faith. It was Martha who went to meet Jesus while Mary remained in the house. In her confession of faith, besides calling Him "Lord," Martha replied with three more Messianic titles: "I believe that You are the Christ, the Son of God, He who is coming into the world." What she failed to understand, as many of us do today, is that Jesus was telling her that the Messianic age had already begun.

"Whoever lives and believes in Me shall never die." Those who believe in Jesus as Savior and Lord already experience eternal life in union with God. It is not necessary to wait for the last day—the resurrection of the dead. For believers eternal life has already begun! But in this world it is only an imperfect experience; the perfect life of righteousness in immortality comes only after the end of time.

Paul says: "Do you not know that all of us who have been

71

baptized into Christ Jesus were baptized into His death? We were buried therefore with Him by baptism into death, so that as Christ was raised from the dead by the glory of the Father, we too might walk in newness of life" (Romans 6:3-4). The newness of life, the joy of the resurrection, is ours every day when we come to Christ in repentance and know His forgiveness. It is a prelude to what is to come.

John 11:20-27

How does your faith in Jesus—His death and resurrection—comfort you in bereavement?

Now is My soul troubled, and what shall I say? "Father, save Me from this hour"?
John 12:27

It was just a few days before Jesus' passion and crucifixion. Among those in Jerusalem attending the feast of the Passover were some Greek proselytes who were allowed only in the Court of the Gentiles in the temple. The events surrounding the Passion are filled with so many references to those who rejected Jesus that we sometimes fail to remember the many pilgrims who believed among both Jews and Gentiles. Several of these Gentile Greeks came to Philip requesting to see and hear more about the Savior.

Jesus replied with a little parable about a grain of wheat. If it does not die, it remains alone. Only if the grain falls into the earth and dies, ceases to exist as grain, will it sprout into a new plant which will bear much fruit. Jesus' death and resurrection were absolutely necessary to win forgiveness of sins for the whole world. God's worldwide kingdom was to come from the new plant rising from the Seed of Abraham after Jesus' burial.

Jesus' question which followed is filled with deep sorrow and sadness: "Now is My soul troubled, and what shall I say? 'Father, save Me from this hour'?" His answer to His own question reveals a faithful Son, obedient to His Father's will: "No, for this purpose I have come to this hour." The Messianic promises in Genesis 3:15 and Genesis 12:1-3 were about to be fulfilled. God's covenant with Abraham has reached its goal: "In you all the families of the earth shall be blessed."

The poignant disquiet in Jesus' question can be comprehended only if we realize the significance of Jesus' atonement. Jesus' voluntary, lifelong self-sacrifice was not an easy submission to the will of the Father but the soul-shaking, tormented, apprehensive obedience of a Son totally committed to His Father's will, absolutely trusting in His Father's promises.

Jesus' unshakable faith and trust are revealed in His prayer: "Father, glorify Thy name." His Father answered just as He did at Jesus' baptism and transfiguration: "I have glorified it, and I will glorify it again." With bold conviction Jesus spoke to the crowd: "Now is the judgment of this world, now shall the ruler of this world be cast out; and I, when I am lifted up from the earth, will draw all men to Myself."

John 12:20-33

For what would you be willing to sacrifice your life if it came to that?

Do you think that I cannot appeal to My Father, and He will at once send Me more than twelve legions of angels? But how then should the Scriptures be fulfilled, that it must be so? . . . Have you come out as against a robber, with swords and clubs to capture Me?

Matthew 26:53, 55

Matthew's account of Jesus' betrayal in the garden emphasizes the fact that God was in control—that everything that had happened and would happen was a fulfillment of Scripture.

Jesus confronted the crowds who came for Him with an attitude of controlled power—lordliness, authority, and dignity. There was no evidence of fear or weakness. He rebuked one of His disciples who attacked the slave of the high priest. His trust in His Father, who, if He appealed to Him, would send more than 12 legions of angels is in direct contrast to the helplessness of His disciples. No one—supernatural or mortal—could stop the inexorable chain of events of His Father's redemptive plan.

Surely He has borne our griefs
and carried our sorrows;

Yet we esteemed Him stricken,
    smitten by God, and afflicted.
But He was wounded for our transgressions,
    He was bruised for our iniquities;
upon Him was the chastisement that made us whole,
    and with His stripes we are healed.
All we like sheep have gone astray;
    we have turned every one to his own way;
and the Lord has laid on Him
    the iniquity of us all."

(Isaiah 53:4-6)

The soldiers and temple police approached Him as a robber. Only violent, fanatical rebels or revolutionaries against Rome were treated with such indignity. Jesus had preached openly in public places; He had never urged insurrection against Rome. "But all this has taken place, that the Scriptures of the prophets might be fulfilled."

Therefore I will divide Him a portion with the great,
    and He shall divide the spoil with the strong;
because he poured out His soul to death,
    and was numbered with the transgressors;
yet He bore the sin of many,
    and made intercession for the transgressors.

(Isaiah 53:12)

Jesus' reference to the fulfillment of Scripture was followed by one of the most deeply moving statements of the gospels: "Then all the disciples forsook Him and fled." Zechariah had predicted: "Strike the shepherd, that the sheep may be scattered."

We will not forsake Him, if we continue to rely on the promises of the Father, the strength of Jesus, and the power of His Spirit.

Matthew 26:51-56; John 18:10-11

How do we sometimes treat Jesus as a "robber"?

Why do you ask Me? . . . Why do you strike Me?
John 18:21, 23

Jesus was taken from the Garden of Gethsemane by the temple guards to the home of Annas, one of the high priests. There God's beloved Son, our living Savior, was subjected to interrogation and abuse by the high priest and his officers. It is mind-boggling to try to comprehend such a humiliating situation—the Son of Man, full of grace and truth, coequal with the Father in glory, the Word become flesh, the Redeemer of the world being questioned by a conniving priest about His teaching. But Jesus responded as the Messiah. He challenged the priest whose own sacred Scriptures had prophesied His work: "I have spoken openly to the world. . . . Why do you ask Me?" In Isaiah 48:16 the prophet tells us that "from the beginning I have not spoken in secret." God's Word has always been openly shared with all the world.

Jesus had traveled through Palestine publicly. Nothing that Jesus taught or accomplished in sign or miracle was hidden from the people or their leaders. But the final acts of the priests were carried out with treachery, in secret. What a contrast between Jesus' selfless offering of Himself and the selfish, hypocritical stance of the priests who did not want their power base threatened! One of the officers, apparently because he felt that Jesus' reply was insolent, struck Him.

"Why do you strike Me?" Those words have come down through 2000 years to haunt us today. But, you say, we never strike Jesus. Think again. Do we not strike Jesus when we deny His divinity; when we reject Him as Savior and Lord of our lives; when we do not commit ourselves to active discipleship in the world; when we trade off Jesus' law and commands for the so-called morality of our age; when we fail to speak out against the spiritual, political, and economic oppression of our fellow human beings?

We strike Jesus when we do not take Him seriously or seek His kingdom first; when we fail to share our vast resources with the millions starving throughout the world; when we raise no protest against the sleazy exploitation of sex and violence in the media; when we permit the destruction of the helpless; when we allow politicians to neglect or oppose programs which are absolutely essential for the poor, the one-parent family, the aged, and the handicapped. When we strike Jesus, we face judgment on earth and in heaven; we have rejected our Savior.

John 18:19-23

How can we keep from "striking" Jesus?

The Way
of Discipleship
in the
Kingdom of God

*You are the salt of the earth; but if salt has
lost its taste, how shall its saltness be restored?*

Matthew 5:13

In the warm climate of Palestine salt was as basic to life as the light of the sun and life-giving water. A bag of salt was an extremely valuable commodity, necessary for the preservation of many kinds of foodstuffs. Palestine had an uncertain climate—an adequate food supply had to be preserved and maintained for the time when the rains failed to come and there was little or no natural yield. Improperly preserved food spoiled; it was not fit for use.

Salt was obtained by evaporation from the Dead Sea and from salt deposits and ponds. Consequently it was frequently mixed with sand. If it was carelessly extracted or if it became wet during transportation or in storage, the salt was lost—only the sand remained. Its preservative quality, its saltness, was gone.

As the salt of the earth, Jesus' disciples—and that includes you and me—are commissioned to preserve the "saltness" of God's covenant of grace. On a planet polluted by self-serving, greed, immorality, lust, violence, lack of reverence for life, unethical practices in business and government, quest for power and world domination, and the exploitation of human and natural resources, proclaiming God's grace is an enormous task. But God's world and all of His beloved creatures can be preserved by the salt of Word and sacrament and the commitment of disciples to the cause of Christ.

Discipleship cannot be restricted to local congregations. By expanding our personal spiritual and social ministries we can bring the Gospel to those who have not heard it and we can help relieve the suffering of the lonely, the aged, the hungry, the poor, the bereaved, and all those whose human dignity is threatened.

We are the salt of the earth when our faith and trust in our Savior, and our commitment and obedience to His will that all humanity be saved, is apparent in all our daily contacts! The salt we share is love and understanding, mercy and forgiveness, concern for and involvement with all of our brothers and sisters throughout the world.

Matthew 5:13; Mark 9:49-50; Luke 14:34-35

How do Christians act as a preservative for the world?

If you love those who love you, what reward have you? Do not even the tax collectors do the same? And if you salute only your brethren, what more are you doing than others? Do not even the Gentiles do the same?

Matthew 5:46-47

In the Roman Empire during the time of Jesus there was an elaborate system of taxation. Within the provinces the collection of taxes was auctioned off to financial companies; they in turn sold their rights to many small speculators who collected from the citizens. Among the Jews these were the publicans or tax collectors. Because they demanded exorbitantly high payments in order to gain great profit and to pay off their Roman masters beyond what the empire requested, they were despised and disliked. In fact, they were openly called sinners and ostracized by other Jews.

Under these circumstances Jesus' injunction to "love your enemies" had profound, unsettling meaning. In the old covenant many believed that they were to love only their neighbors, their brethren. They did not feel that their love had to extend to public sinners and to tax collectors who exploited the public. Nevertheless, like all people, tax collectors and Gentiles were capable of warm, loving relationships within their circle of family and friends.

But the love which Jesus demanded is the love that flows from reconciliation to God. It is deeply concerned with the spiritual and physical well-being of every individual—with the promotion of human dignity and worth rather than with social and cultural differences. It is love which causes us to behave toward others and feel for others as God does and Jesus did in His entire life. Jesus' redeeming love was extended to everyone—publican and ruler, slave and master, male and female, widows and orphans, criminals and those who kept the law. He loved those who responded to His reconciling love with the love of commitment and discipleship. He loved those who rejected and persecuted Him. His prayers and concern were for all.

For us as disciples, reconciling love is an expression of our personal relationship to God. To experience such love is to give love. To know forgiveness is to grant forgiveness. To realize Jesus' self-sacrifice on the cross is to sacrifice oneself in service to humanity. To follow Jesus is to rely on God's grace, to pray for strength to do His will, to have complete and absolute faith and trust in His steadfast love. Then we are able to share God's goodness and perfection within the Christian community and to the ends of the world!

Matthew 5:43-48

Who are the "enemies" Jesus asks you to love in our world?

Is not life more than food, and the body more than clothing? Look at the birds of the air. . . . Are you not of more value than they? And which of you by being anxious can add one cubit to his span of life? And why are you anxious about clothing? . . . But If God so clothes the grass of the field, which today is alive and tomorrow is thrown into the oven, will He not much more clothe you, O men of little faith?

Matthew 6:25-30

The Sermon on the Mount immediately followed Jesus' call to Peter, Andrew, James, and John to be "fishers of men." It is addressed to the new disciples and the crowds who followed Him—the disciples whose responsibility it would be to teach others the way of life in the kingdom of God.

Discipleship must be the overriding concern of every person who follows Jesus. It dare not be diminished by worry over the problems of everyday living. Jesus forbids anxiety: "Do not be anxious about your life, what you shall eat or what you shall drink, nor about your body, what you shall put on." The Father's care for the birds of the air, the lilies of the field, and the grasses of the meadows, and their utter dependence on God, is to show us how much God cares for us. He gave us our intricately designed bodies and His magnificent creation with everything in it needed to sustain life; He gave us new, spiritual life in His kingdom through the life, death, and resurrection of His beloved Son—we are clothed in forgiveness and righteousness. All we need do is to believe and trust in God's infinite love and concern for us.

Anxiety blinds us to the magnitude of God's love and care. It destroys faith and trust in God's grace. It caters to dependence on self instead of dependence on our Savior. It can even erode our sense of responsibility in discipleship. But if we depend on God for our physical and spiritual needs, there is nothing we cannot do (Philippians 4:13). God can always be trusted. "Therefore do not be anxious about tomorrow, for tomorrow will be anxious for itself."

Matthew 6:24-34

How do we show that we really and truly depend on God? How do we acknowledge it?

Why do you see the speck that is in your brother's eye, but do not notice the log that is in your own eye? Or how can you say to your brother, "Let me take the speck out of your eye," when there is the log in your own eye?

Matthew 7:3-4

Jesus taught His disciples with concepts they were able to understand. His admonition against judging others, the log and the speck, was similar to one they had learned from the rabbis. The rabbis also warned against judging one's brother. Each one was to think kindly about the other. Jesus was warning His disciples against the self-righteous judgment which could blind them to the depth of their own sin. Hypocrisy is oftentimes a cover-up of one's own disharmony with God.

The Great Commisson, "Go, and make disciples of all nations, baptizing them . . . and teaching them . . . all that I have commanded you," can be accomplished only with a diversity of disciples able to reach out to the inner city, suburbia, and rural areas. In our complex society it is often impossible to discern the effectiveness of mission immediately. Disciples are not to judge one another either for style of service or personality.

To see a "speck" in the eye of another is to sin against him and against God. The "log" in our own eye can blind us to the fact that we sin against God when we judge another; our foolish judgment may destroy one's mission. That must never happen! It is necessary always to look at ourselves truthfully, to see that we serve in a community of sinners and saints. In Romans 2:1 Paul says: "Therefore you have no excuse, O man, whoever you are, when you judge another; for in

81

passing judgment upon him you condemn yourself, because you, the judge, are doing the very same things."

There is an Indian proverb which says, "Do not judge your brother until you have walked a mile in his moccasins." We cannot begin to know another's fears and apprehensions, strengths and weaknesses. We need to give encouragement, to show mercy, kindness, and love to all our fellow disciples. We dare not be guilty of fault-finding, condemnation, or self-righteous criticism, which can undermine the effectiveness of discipleship. We dare not add one tiny "speck" to another's burden.

Repentance is the only way to remove the "log" that blinds us to the needs of others. Then comes the joy and gratitude of forgiveness.

Matthew 7:1-5; Luke 6:37-42; Romans 2:1-11

What does judging mean? What does it include? Are there ever times when we must make judgments? When?

Or what man of you, if his son asks him for bread, will give him a stone? Or if he asks for a fish, will give him a serpent?

Matthew 7:9-10

The disciple in the kingdom of God is the most precious possession of our Father in heaven—a Father who wants us to come to Him in prayer, a Father who shows us infinitely more love and compassion and forgiveness than our human fathers. To teach this eternal truth, Jesus emphasized the importance of persistent prayer. Prayer was the very essence of His faith and trust in His Father. He lived His whole life in communion with God. He showed us that our God is a loving Father, who invites His beloved children to speak to Him openly and unashamedly. "Ask, and it will be given you; seek, and you will find; knock, and it will be opened to you." God hears; He listens, and He acts.

Jesus is greatly concerned that each of us trust the Father as He did. Therefore He asked: "Or what man of you, if his son asks him for bread, will given him a stone? Or if he asks for a fish, will give him a serpent?" Jesus makes a comparison with a human father. If such a sinful human father takes so seriously the request of a child for bread and fish that it would be unconscionable for him to substitute a useless stone or a dangerous serpent, how much more will our holy God "give good things to those who ask Him"! "Every good endowment and every perfect gift is from above, coming down from the Father of lights with whom there is no variation or shadow due to change," (James 1:17). The good things which the Father never holds back, which He offers freely and generously, are His unending love and grace.

In the early church, bread and fish were symbolic of the Lord's Supper, in which there is forgiveness of sins, life, and salvation. These are the good and perfect gifts for which we yearn and for which we pray—although sometimes we find it difficult to put into words. Perhaps we do not understand or we do not trust God enough or we believe that tangibles we can see and feel are more important than the intangible peace which is never denied us.

"Likewise the Spirit helps us in our weakness; for we do not know how to pray as we ought, but the Spirit Himself intercedes for us with sighs too deep for words. And He who searches the hearts of men knows what is the mind of the Spirit, because the Spirit intercedes for the saints according to the will of God."

Matthew 7:7-11; Luke 11:9-13; Romans 8:18-30

What does prayer mean in your life?

O man of little faith, why did you doubt?
Matthew 14:31

After the feeding of the 5000 Jesus directed His disciples to get into their boat and go to Bethsaida on the other side of the Sea of Galilee. He remained behind. Very early in the morning the winds came up with fury and the sea became extremely rough. The disciples were unable to make any headway in the face of the powerful wind. They were terrified, alone on the raging sea.

From the hills on the far side of the lake Jesus perceived their plight, and He came to them over the water. When they saw Him, the disciples were even more terrified, for they thought He was a ghost. But Jesus spoke to them, "It is I; have no fear." With his usual impulsiveness and an added measure of audacity, Peter said to Jesus, "Lord, if it is You, bid me come to You on the water." Impetuous Peter certainly did not think before he spoke; nor did he perceive what the consequence of his action might be. But when Jesus called to him, Peter left the boat and started to walk toward Him. In the face of the strong wind his brash courage left him and his faith declined. He sank into the water. In his distress he cried out to Jesus to save him. Jesus reached out and caught him saying, "O man of little faith, why did you doubt?" They got into the boat; the wind stopped blowing, and the sea became calm.

Peter's reactions are the reactions of all disciples, though we prefer not to admit it. Courage and cowardice, thankfulness and thoughtlessness, faith and doubt are opposing qualities that we all exhibit on various occasions.

But Peter's time and our time are eons apart. Faith is indeed tried in an age where wisdom and intellect, computers and statistics, power and force are almost deified. The idea of trusting in a God whom one cannot see is often scoffed at and ridiculed. Fear of ostracism for one's faith, the emphasis on self-reliance, the pull of materialism, anxiety and worry—all these diminish faith and trust. Christ deals with doubt and offers to replace it with trust and confidence. He offers to share His power with His followers. He extends His reliable promises and guarantees them with the seal of His resurrection. Without Him we can do nothing. But *with* God all things are possible. Even faith!

Matthew 14:22-33.

Why do you doubt? How would you act if you did not doubt?

What do you think Simon? From whom do kings of the earth take toll or tribute? From their sons or from others?

Matthew 17:25

Taxation has always been a prime subject for debate, usually quite heated.

The Roman Empire sprawled acrcross the ancient world of Jesus' time. All the nations which Rome had conquered and colonized, including Palestine, had to pay tribute to Caesar. The appointed leader of each conquered province had to levy taxes on the subject people. But Roman citizens did not have to pay taxes.

There was another tax peculiar only to the Jews—the temple tax. Every male Jew 20 years of age and over was obligated to pay a yearly tax to the temple authorities of one-half shekel, equivalent to two day's pay. In early March an announcement was made in the villages that the tax was due. On the 15th of March booths were set up in each village for the tax collectors. The money was needed to support the functions of the temple, for upkeep, and for the robes and appointments of the priests. No one was exempt; rich and poor alike paid the tax.

When Jesus and His disciples came to Capernaum, one of the tax collectors came to Peter and asked whether Jesus paid the temple tax. Peter said He did. Jesus, however, saw a lesson in the occasion. He asked Peter: "What do you think, Simon? From whom do kings . . . take toll or tribute? From their sons or from others?" Perhaps, since Peter replied that the king's sons did not pay tax, Jesus was pointing out that, as God's Son, He should be exempt from the temple tax—as should the disciples, who were the children of their King. But He quickly insisted that the disciples pay the tax in order not to cause offense.

This story, together with the one which admonishes us to give Caesar his due, reminds us that Christians have an obligation to the state as well as the church.

Christians are citizens of two states—the kingdom of God and the secular nation. Therefore we should willingly and gratefully assume our responsibility to the nation both as a duty and as an example to those who would defraud the government and attempt to avoid their obligation. It is essential that citizens of the kingdom of God witness to their membership in that kingdom by paying taxes and supporting the efforts of the secular body in its service to the citizenry.

Matthew 17:24-27

Should churches be taxed or be exempt from taxation? How do you feel about using the label "church" or "religious organization" to avoid taxation?

Have you not read that He who made them from the beginning made them male and female, and said, "For this reason a man shall leave his father and mother and be joined to his wife, and the two shall become one flesh"?

Matthew 19:4-5

Jesus was constantly being tested by His enemies in the hope that He would make a compromising statement that they could use against Him. Their question, "Is it lawful to divorce one's wife for any cause?" was one such attempt to discredit Him. His answer went directly to the beginning of sacred Scripture—the account of the creation of mankind in Genesis.

By the time of Jesus two schools of interpretation of the law had become dominant in Judaism. The school of Shammai was strict; adultery was the only ground for divorce. The school of Hillel was extremly liberal; a man could divorce his wife if she burned his dinner or spoke to men on the street or failed to tie up her hair properly or showed disrespect for her parents or if her husband wanted a more attractive wife.

Under rabbinic law a woman had very little social or legal status; she was in many ways denied the dignity of being a person.

The Book of Genesis, however, reveals a far different attitude. Man and woman, lovingly created in the image of God, are both equal and precious in His sight, capable of communion with Him and capable of living in harmony with Him and with their fellow human beings. God's love becomes visible in loving human relationships. Companionship, forgiveness, and reconciling love, therefore, are all part of the marriage bond as God intended it. The love of a husband for his wife should be a caring, sacrificial, serving love. The same is true of the love of a wife for her husband. Marriage is a communion of two persons concerned not only with physical union but with the union of minds and spirits, willing to share together in the accomplishment of God's purpose for all mankind.

Jesus' emphasis on the profound spiritual truths about the marriage relationship lifts woman to the highest ideal as a person, precious to God, beloved by Him, created in His image, and redeemed by Him.

Matthew 19:3-9; Mark 10:11-12;
Genesis 1:27-28; 2:18-24; Ephesians 5:21-33

Are there justifiable reasons for divorce? What about remarriage after divorce?

Why do you ask Me about what is good?
Matthew 19:17

A young ruler came to Jesus inquiring about what good deed he must do in order to have eternal life, to be part of the kingdom of God, to have peace with God. His question indicates that he must have had some reservations about his relationship with God.

Jesus' question and reply let the young man know right away that it is impossible for any human being to attain the goodness of or perfection of God.

Jesus' command that he keep the Law was entirely fitting in light of the young man's self-righteous background; he actually believed he was keeping the Law.

The commandments which Jesus cited from the Second Tablet of the Law and from Leviticus had to do with relationships among people and with each one's responsibility for the welfare of others. To the young man's inquiry about what he still lacked, Jesus replied: "If you would be perfect, go, sell what you possess and give to the poor, and you will have treasure in heaven; and come, follow Me." The young man left in sorrow. He could not comply with Jesus' suggestion. Riches had become his idol.

Unfortunately, the sad young man's outward conformance to the Law blinded him to the fact that he really put his trust in his material possessions rather than God. Jesus was asking him to prove his faith in God by putting aside his idol, his riches. Jesus is reminding us that we enter the kingdom of God only when we follow Him exclusively, with "no other gods before Him." It means being committed to doing the will of the Father. Jesus' demands were far greater than the young man anticipated. They required a complete change of commitment.

There is a "goodness" that only God and His perfect Son inherently possess. It is total righteousness and holiness. Another rich man—Abraham—believed in the Messiah—and God reckoned that faith in him as righteousness, a garment that clothed him in perfection in the eyes of God, because it was the spotless righteousness of the perfect Son. By His question Jesus was forcing the rich young ruler to look for goodness outside himself and his own potential. The answer to Christ's question lies in the nature of the Person asking the question.

Matthew 19:16-22; Mark 10:17-22; Luke 18:18-23

What do you think "good" means? Can you do good? Of what benefit is it to do so?

What do you think? . . .
Which of the two did the will of the father?
Matthew 21:28, 31

In the parable of the two sons Jesus confronted the chief priests and elders with their rejection of the authority of John the Baptist. The story has great significance for us today.

There were two sons whose father came to them, requesting that they work in his vineyard. The first said, "I will not," but afterward he repented and worked for his father. The second said, "I will," but he did not go to work. Which one did his father's will?

When John the Baptist came preaching: "Repent, for the kingdom of heaven is at hand," many sinners came to him for baptism, confessing their sins and repenting. But the priests and elders did not believe in John's prophetic ministry. They saw no need to change or to acknowledge that the Messiah had come.

According to Jesus, the first son's "I will not" symbolized sinners, tax collectors, and prostitutes, who could change under the influence of God's Spirit. The second son's "I will" represented the leaders whose self-righteous concern for form and ritual paid no regard to their need of a Savior.

Among Christians are those who come into sanctuaries to worship but whose cloak of respectability and outward piety cover up a self-righteous pride which will not confess to their need of a Savior. Therefore they do not really hear the Gospel. The words of confession and forgiveness, the prayers and hymns are empty and meaningless rote because they are not followed by contrition and humble service to other sinners. On the other hand, there are those who claim that they want no part of religion or the organized church. Yet they may come to repentance and be saved by God's grace.

We all have deep-seated spiritual needs. Sometimes it is easier for a so-called irreligious person to see his need for repentance and forgiveness than it is for one who feels he has it made with God. Without repentance, piety and respectability are nothing. It is absolutely essential for every person to see himself as a sinner in need of repentance and forgiveness; only then can he believe in the Savior and do the Father's will.

Matthew 21:28-32; 3:1-12

How do you do the will of the Father?

Why put Me to the test, you hypocrites? . . . Whose likeness and inscription is this?
Matthew 22:18-20

Those among the Pharisees who opposed Jesus were unrelenting in their determination to trap Him somehow so they could accuse Him of sedition before both Jewish and Roman authorities. Along with some supporters of Herod, they plotted to test Him with a question about the annual poll tax. Every person who lived under Roman rule was obligated to pay the tax to Rome. The Pharisees themselves were opposed to paying the tax; although, to keep their status, they routinely did so. The Herodians, who collaborated with Rome, favored paying the tax for their own security. Both parties felt that Jesus was a threat both to the religious hierarchy and the Roman government.

Their question, "Is it lawful to pay taxes to Caesar, or not?" was designed to entrap Jesus. If He replied that the tax should be paid, He would lose credibility with the mass of Jewish people, who detested Roman domination. Among the Jews was a party of Zealot nationalists who opposed the tax and refused to pay it because they felt that only God was their king; their allegiance was only to Him. If Jesus replied that the tax should not be paid, He could have been brought before the Jewish leaders as well as the Roman authorities for inciting resistance to the established government. It was a no-win situation.

Their ploy was too crude to trap Jesus. He merely asked to see a coin used to pay the tax. "Whose likeness and inscription is this?" When they answered, "Caesar's," He said to them: "Render therefore to Caesar the things that are Caesar's, and to God the things that are God's." His forthright answer could not be contested by either party. The antagonists retreated.

In answering the question, Jesus proclaimed that our obligation to state and national government does not contradict our duty to carry out God's will. In spiritual matters the kingdom of God is supreme. Both Pharisees and Herodians knew that the rabbis taught that the existing government must be obeyed.

It is essential that Christians intelligently and responsibly involve themselves in political issues by availing themselves of their right to vote, by exemplary and honest service in political office, and by supporting laws and programs that promote the welfare of all citizens.

Matthew 22:15-22; Mark 12:13-17; Luke 20:19-26

How do you interpret separation of church and state?

Is a lamp brought in to be put under a bushel, or under a bed, and not on a stand?
Mark 4:21-23

The pottery oil lamp used in Palestinian homes was one of its most important furnishings. It was a small, round bowl with a pinched lip or spout at one end for the flax wick which rested in a pool of olive oil contained in the lamp. Every home had at least one lamp. In a simple home it was placed in a niche in the wall or on an overturned earthenware vessel, the bushel. A wealthy family might have a bronze lamp and lampstand.

The lamp was kept burning constantly. Its wick was frequently trimmed to keep it bright. During the day it gave light to the house which, for poor families, usually was a single room with a very small window high on the wall. At night the light of the burning lamp was believed to ward off evil spirits. In the morning it was used to rekindle the cooking fire. A reserve supply of oil was stored in a jar.

Jesus said: "You are the light of the world. A city set on a hill cannot be hid. Nor do men light a lamp and put it under a bushel, but on a stand, and it gives light to the house. Let your light so shine before men, that they may see your good works and give glory to your Father who is in heaven."

Discipleship, like the oil lamp, must always "shine." It is not a one-hour-a-week witness to a congregation that we believe. Its witness must go into businesses, factories, hospitals, nursing homes, offices, and recreaton areas. It is vital to the interpersonal relationships in our homes for forgiveness, for teaching, for helping each other, and for sharing joys and sorrows.

Discipleship doesn't just happen. It must be cared for like the ancient oil lamp. It must be trimmed and replenished by the Gospel, sustained by the sacraments, refreshed by the love and fellowship of other Christians. Pottery is fragile; it must be handled carefully so it does not break and the light go out. Discipleship is fragile, too. We must guard against the pull of materialism, which can keep us from worship, meditation, and study; against the distortion and rationalization of doctrine which caters to self-righteousness; and against substituting self-glorifying "good works" for the responsibility of selfless service and mission.

Keeping our light bright and shining is not a difficult task, for we have the "Light of the world," whose love and light will always rekindle our lamp when it fails.

Mark 4:21-23; Matthew 5:14-16; Luke 8:16; 11:33.

What is the relationship between your faith, your light, and the good works which Jesus demands?

What were you discussing on the way?
Mark 9:33

Jesus knows us—our pride and ambition, our desires and dreams. He also knew His disciples. He knew them before He called them.

Jesus had instructed His disciples on the way to Capernaum that soon the Son of Man would be put to death but would rise on the third day. They did not understand. The charisma of their Teacher, His ability to draw huge crowds so eager to hear the truth, His miracles of healing, feeding, and calming the raging storms awakened expectations of a political kingdom in which they could serve as princes or lords. They even dreamed about throwing off the yoke of mighty Rome, even though Jesus' followers, for the most part, were not army generals, politicians, industrialists, wealthy patrons, or even ordinary soldiers who could war against the mighty Caesar and win! They were poor pilgrims earnestly yearning for the truth about God, His forgiveness and reconciliation—the peace that passes all understanding which remains through the rise and fall of kingdoms and nations.

"What were you discussing on the way?" The disciples remained silent; they were ashamed to admit that they had been discussing who was the greatest. What a contrast to Jesus' totally selfless love! Jesus' only ambition was to do His Father's will, to seek out and serve the lost, the sorrowful, and the poor in spirit.

True greatness in the kingdom of God is humble service. It is like serving and loving a child who can give nothing in return except love—no political favor or material reward. To receive a child, to selflessly care for such a "little one"—or anyone who is not mature in faith—is to receive Jesus and the Father.

Ambition in secular and religious life is not wrong in itself. It is wrong when the ambitious one desires to dominate other persons, to have power over those less fortunate than himself, to deny their human dignity. That is a denial of discipleship. To serve in God's kingdom is to forget self as Jesus did, to be concerned about the reconciliation of all His children.

Mark 9:33-37; Matthew 18:1-5; Luke 9:46-48

Contrast the way of discipleship in the kingdom of God—your own personal mission—with the demands of the secular world. What conflicts do you encounter?

Can a blind man lead a blind man?
Will they not both fall into a pit?
Luke 6:39

In the Great Commission, Jesus spells out clearly the way of discipleship: "Go therefore and make disciples of all nations, baptizing them in the name of the Father and of the Son and of the Holy Spirit, teaching them to observe all that I have commanded you; and lo, I am with you always, to the close of the age." The 12 disciples whom Jesus chose and who followed Him during His lifetime were exposed to the pure Word of God, Jesus Himself. They witnessed His example, teaching, signs and miracles—yet they often misunderstood His Gospel of love and forgiveness; they often failed to perceive the meaning of disicpleship.

In His little parable of the blind leading the blind, Jesus is sharing a profound truth—that teaching and learning and understanding are essential to effective and productive discipleship, and that the disicple "when he is fully taught will be like his teacher." We dare not take lightly Jesus' injunction. His question tells us very plainly that a guide is responsible for the spiritual well-being of those whom he leads; if he misleads them, they will all fall into judgment.

We have so much more than did the disciples of Jesus' time: the Word of God as revealed in the Bible; the Living Word who came to die for us in self-sacrifice and rose from the dead; the Spirit of Truth; the sacraments; and the wisdom of the saints who have preceded us.

There are many blind guides today who would have us stray from the spiritual truths which are our heritage. There are secularists who would have us believe that faith and self-denial are outmoded concepts. There are cults that attempt to manipulate people and sometimes even succeed in infiltrating government, cults whose morality and ethics serve only their own prejudices. There are those whose self-centered ideas dilute the responsibility to be in service to all humankind everywhere on our planet. There are humanists who emphasize the superiority of man, his philantrophy and idealism, but who deny the divinity of Christ. We must not allow ourselves to be swayed by any of them.

Luke 6:39-40; Matthew 15:13-14; 28:18-20

What "blind guides" do you see in the world today? How can we keep ourselves and our children from being deceived by them?

Why do you call Me "Lord, Lord,"
and not do what I tell you?

Luke 6:46

To call Jesus "Savior" is to acknowledge Him as our Redeemer who frees us from God's condemnation; to call Jesus "Lord" is to follow Him in obedient discipleship. Those who call Jesus "Lord" in reverence and faith are those who do the will of the Father; they are both hearers and doers of Jesus' words.

In the early Christian church and during the time of Jesus' ministry there were those who called Jesus "Lord" out of respect for Him as a great teacher, to show loyalty to the one they called Messiah, or to pay homage to a risen King. It was also a term used in worship. But to call Jesus "Lord" from one's heart is to confess that He is God and that only He can forgive sin; it is a mighty confession of faith! It is to proclaim to the world that Jesus is Lord of heaven and earth and, more personally, Lord of our lives—new life built on a foundation of faith, committed to the words of Jesus.

Jesus likens one who hears and does His words to the man who built the foundation of his house on rock. The man who digs deeply and builds his house on bedrock never need fear the ravages of flooding—his house stands firm. But the man who digs no foundation and simply builds his house on the sandy surface will lose it when the storms and floods batter it—it will not stand. Anyone who has lived in the desert knows how a dry, sandy wash can become a raging torrent with immense power when the rains come. Anyone who has lived close to a river knows how devastating floods can be during seasons of deluge.

Faith is like those houses. It must be deeply implanted and allowed to grow strong and firm so that it cannot be torn down and battered during times of temptation and crisis. We are all subject to temptation, despair, loneliness, and sorrow. Those with superficial faith have little resistance to these very human experiences. Faith needs to be nurtured by hearing the Word in church and home, by partaking of the Sacrament, by sharing doubts and sorrows and disappointments, by being open and receptive to the love and concern of other Christians, by allowing God's Spirit to move within us as He strives to keep us in the true faith. That faith leads to cheerful obedience.

Luke 6:46-49; Matthew 7:21-27

How do you confess, testify, and show that Jesus is Lord of your life?

If then you have not been faithful in the unrighteous mammon, who will entrust to you the true riches? And if you have not been faithful in that which is another's, who will give you that which is your own?

Luke 16:11-12

Absentee landlordism was common in Palestine. Large estates belonging to wealthy persons were run by stewards who usually were quite trustworthy. This was not the case in the parable of the dishonest steward which preceded Jesus' question.

It was brought to the attention of a rich man that his steward was wasting his goods. He immediately asked for an accounting from the steward; he also dismissed him. The steward was faced with a crisis whose solution demanded some quick thinking. He felt he was not strong enough to go out digging in the fields; furthermore, his pride would not allow it. He felt it was necessary to win friends in the community who might be useful to him later. Therefore he called his master's debtors and drastically reduced the amount they owed.

The entire transaction was totally dishonest. The steward certainly was not trustworthy in handling his master's goods.

Jesus taught His disciples that anyone who could not be trusted with handling goods and money, particularly another's, could not be trusted to share God's grace. Devotion to money and riches which tempts a person to falsify records, charge exorbitant interest, cheat on taxes, and hoard far more than he needs is not compatible with devotion to God and with His will for our lives and the lives of those to whom we witness.

"The true riches" are reconciliation with God, forgiveness, and service in His kingdom. Spiritual values—peace, hope, and joy—are far more important than the accumulation of worldly wealth.

Luke 16:1-13; Matthew 6:24

Is it really possible to serve both God and mammon? How does God expect us to use our salary and possessions?

Were not ten cleansed? Where are the nine? Was no one found to return and give praise to God except this foreigner?

Luke 17:17

Jesus was on His way to Jerusalem. He passed between Samaria and Galilee, and as He approached a village, He was stopped by ten lepers. Nine were Jews; one was a Samaritan.

Lepers were considered to be ritually unclean. They were socially ostracized, deprived of the companionship of family and friends, companions only to other lepers and outcasts. Some authorities would not allow a leper within 50 yeards of a village, especially if the wind were blowing their way. Lepers were totally isolated and alone. They could not even worship in the synagogue or temple.

It is ironic that in Luke's story of the ten lepers he points out that one of them was a Samaritan. Samaritans were also rejected by Palestinian Jews as outcasts, part Jews, foreigners. But here the common tragedy of suffering and disease brought together Jew and Samaritan.

The lepers asked Jesus for mercy. Jesus told them to go and show themselves to the priests. If the priests acknowledged the cleansing and healing of the disease, and if the one who was cleansed gave a suitable offering, he was then allowed to join the religious and social community. The lepers obeyed Jesus. On the way to see the priests they were healed. The nine Jewish lepers continued on their way. But when the Samaritan saw that he was healed, he immediately returned to Jesus to thank Him.

It is significant that only he returned to give praise and thanksgiving to Jesus for his healing. He recognized Jesus as God; his faith was the kind that serves God in gratitude for healing and forgiveness. Forgiveness is inherent in many of Jesus' healing miracles. This story indirectly indicates that the kingdom of God is not to be exclusive. It was to be open to everyone—Gentiles and Jews.

The primary lesson, however, is gratitude for God's grace. There are many of us today who suffer from the same ingratitude as the nine lepers. We often fail to recognize that we are actually healed—and if by chance we do, we take it for granted. We fail to acknowledge the One who is responsible for the healing. We give honor and praise to physicians, nurses, technicians, and pharmacists yet fail to recognize and thank Him who is the source of intellect, wisdom, and skill, and the primary source of the healing. Like the Samaritan leper, our daily thanks for health and healing should be directed to Him "who heals *all* our diseases," physical and spiritual.

Luke 17:11-19

How does this story of healing apply to us today?

Do you also wish to go away?
John 6:67

Jesus had come to the end of his Galilean ministry. When He left Galilee to return to Jerusalem, it was to face the horror of His passion and crucifixion.

There had been a change of attitude toward Jesus among many of the disciples who followed Him. They were unable to accept His teaching, perhaps because they did not understand, or perhaps because they were unable to fulfill the demands of discipleship. For whatever reason, they "no longer went about with Him." To "go about with" meant far more than the physical following of Jesus. It meant to be devoted to Jesus as a disciple or servant is to a master. It meant faith and trust, willingness to follow, even to Jersualem. Only the 12 loyal disciples remained.

Jesus' question to His 12 friends, "Do you also wish to go away?" is filled with pathos. Peter answered for all of them, "Lord, to whom shall we go? You have the words of eternal life; and we have believed, and have come to know, that You are the Holy One of God." What an absolute, unequivocal witness and confession of faith! To see Jesus as Savior is a very personal perception—to know one's own forgiveness. But to confess that Jesus is "Lord" and "the Holy One of God" is to acknowledge that He is Ruler of the entire creation, the King of kings and the Lord of lords. To call Jesus by these titles is to recognize Him as the living, incarnate Word—God! It is Jesus who restores us to harmony with God, with our fellow persons, and with the natural creation. It is Jesus who calls us to serve in His kingdom here and now while we are still in our secular world.

The constancy of discipleship—which is essential for effective witnessing—is not our work; it is always God's work, a gift of His

97

grace and steadfast love. He calls us in Baptism, enlightens us with His Spirit, brings us to faith, sustains us through His Word and the Lord's Supper so that we can live a godly life on earth now and in eternity forever. Thanksgiving for the peace of forgiveness, the joy of reconciliation, and the hope of resurrection—this is the motivation for a lifetime of discipleship in the kingdom of God.

John 6:66-71

How does one remain constant in discipleship?

Do you know what I have done to you?
John 13:12

Jesus' public ministry was at an end. He had come to Jerusalem to face the Passion—His cup of woe that included rejection, terrible loneliness, the humiliation of a public trial as a common criminal, and the indescribable mental and physical agony of crucifixion. He knew what He had to do; yet even in His sorrow and weariness of spirit He felt deep compassion for the city which had failed to recognize Him as Lord. And He wept. "O Jerusalem, Jerusalem, killing the prophets and stoning those who are sent to you! How often would I have gathered your children together as a hen gathers her brood under her wings, and you would not!" Jerusalem did not understand His message of reconciliation, repentance, and forgiveness. The exultant cries of "Blessed is He who comes in the name of the Lord" would soon become the hate-filled shout, "Crucify Him!" Even His own disciples did not comprehend His ministry, His Messianic mission.

In an upper room in the city, provided by one of His many nameless friends, Jesus gathered His disciples together for His last supper with them. It was Jewish custom to wash the feet of those who entered the home, as an act of hospitality. Water was commonly used, but on ceremonial occasions it could be done with oil. This task was ordinarily performed by a slave—preferably a Gentile one. It was considered a demeaning job, beneath the dignity of a male Jew. Apparently none of the disciples could bring himself to perform the task.

To the great consternation of His disciples, Jesus left His supper and knelt down to wash the feet—one after the other—of His beloved companions. Only voluble Peter protested. The others were too stunned to react.

"Do you know what I have done to you?" comes from the very depth of Jesus' soul. Do we really understand that in the kingdom of God the way of discipleship is humble sacrificial service to all of humanity, those for whom Jesus came in humility and those for whom He died in humility, including the hungry, the thirsty, the naked, the lonely, the ill, the imprisoned, the unloved, the poor, and the outcast?

John 13:1-17; Luke 13:34; 22:24-27

What is your conception of discipleship in light of Jesus' question? What are the opportunities for personal, congregational, and community service right around your home and church?

Woman, why are you weeping? Whom do you seek?
John 20:15

The tomb was empty! The earlier excitement at finding the stone rolled away and of running to tell Peter and John was gone. Mary Magdalene returned in anguish and sorrow to the empty tomb, looking for the body of the crucified Jesus. She saw Jesus in the garden but did not recognize Him.

Mary Magdalene was the first person to see the empty tomb. She was also the first person to see the risen Christ. But because her focus was entirely on an empty tomb and the body of a dearly beloved friend, she could not comprehend the significance of the resurrection event. Mary believed that Jesus' body had been carried away— perhaps to a final resting place. Her grief prevented her from discerning the resurrected Jesus. Even when He asked, "Why are you weeping? Whom do you seek?" she did not know Him. Presuming Him to be the gardener, she said, "Sir, if you have carried Him away, tell me where you have laid Him, and I will take Him away." Her preoccupation with death kept her from seeing the only real Life that matters.

In deep and poignant compassion, Jesus said, "Mary." Her blindness disappeared; Mary recognized her risen Lord—triumphant over death! The grave could not hold Him! Death had not conquered Him! It is significant that even after His death and resurrection Jesus still seeks us out and calls those whom He loves—and He will continue to do so. He speaks to us through God's Holy Spirit—calling us away from an empty tomb to the glory of our risen Savior.

Mary's joy at seeing and recognizing that Jesus was really and truly alive could not be kept to herself. She ran to tell the disciples, "I have seen the Lord." What a tremendous witness! To believe in Jesus was to believe that the man who had lived and worked and talked and befriended outcasts and sinners was the Son of God! He was the same Jesus she had known; He was also the risen Christ, God's Son. "No one has ever seen God; the only Son, who is in the bosom of the Father, He has made Him known" (John 1:18).

John 20:1-18

What kind of weeping does the risen Christ remove from our life?

Have you believed because you have seen Me?
John 20:29

Thomas was not with the disciples when Jesus appeared to them on Easter evening. He refused to believe them when they told him that they had seen their Lord: "Unless I see in His hands the print of the nails, and place my finger in the mark of the nails, and place my hand in His side, I will not believe." For Thomas, seeing was believing.

Eight days later all of the disciples, including Thomas, were in a room with the doors closed. Suddenly there was Jesus right in the room with them, offering them freely God's gift of grace—the peace of reconciliation. To Thomas He gave an invitation: "Put your finger here, and see My hands; and put out your hand, and place it in My side; do not be faithless, but believing." Thomas immediately became aware that he was in the presence of the living God. "My Lord and my God!" is a powerful confession of faith.

"In the beginning was the Word, . . . and the Word was God. . . . To all who received Him, who believed in His name, He gave power to become children of God; who were born, not of blood nor of the will of the flesh nor of the will of man, but of God. . . . And from His fulness have we all received, grace upon grace." Whether one physically sees or not is unimportant; it is God's Holy Spirit who gives us the gift of spiritual perception, which recognizes Jesus as the Incarnate Word of God.

It was Thomas who earlier had realized the fate of Jesus, and who had encouraged the disciples to go on to Jersualem when they were filled with fear about their safety: "Let us also go, that we may die with Him" (John 11:16). Jesus' humiliation, suffering, and death apparently triggered doubt and skepticism among the disciples. This we can surely understand, because each one of us is a doubting Thomas by nature. To be able to confess as Thomas did is a gift of the Holy Spirit.

We did not actually see the humiliation and crucifixion as Thomas did. We have the witness of the gospels—we know that it happened. It is a historical fact. There are other, more subtle influences which tempt us to doubt. The apathy of many Christians, their rejection of the way of discipleship, the attraction of worldly possessions and pleasures, the dogma of self-awareness and self-fulfillment with its emphasis on self-reliance—all these can be very attractive rationalizations for skepticism. They can blind us to the truth. They can divert us from the demands and responsibility of discipleship.

"Without having seen Him you love Him; though you do not now see Him you believe in Him and rejoice with unutterable and exalted joy" (1 Peter 1:8).

John 20:24-29; 1:1-18

What causes you to doubt? How do you deal with it?

Simon, son of John, do you love Me more than these?
John 21:15-17

Three times Jesus addressed a poignant question to Peter: "Do you love Me?" Brash, self-confident, bold Peter was being forced by the resurrected Christ to look at himself. Peter had always been the first discile to loudly proclaim his loyalty to Jesus. He was also the first to recognize Jesus as the Messiah, the Savior of the world. He was also the first to publicly deny Jesus, the first to fail to confess his

101

Lord in a time of crisis.

Peter's answers to the first two questions indicate that he was aware of Jesus' intimate knowledge of him: "Yes, Lord; You know that I love You." He was grieved that Jesus would repeat the question a third time—and his answer changed: "Lord, *You know everything;* You know that I love You." Certainly Peter remembered the awful anguish, the utter despair, and the terrible loneliness he suffered after he denied his Savior. His answer is an admission that Jesus really knew everything about him—his faith, his doubts, his weakness, his pride, his sinfulness. It was a humble confession of repentance and faith. Peter's self-reliance was gone, replaced by the awareness that he needed Jesus, that he was unable to serve Him unless he relied wholly on his Savior. His confession of love was, therefore, a commitment to service, to discipleship—to "Feed My sheep" and to "Follow Me."

Peter was not alone in his denial of Christ; we all share in that act. Failure to witness to God's saving grace in word and deed is also a denial of Christ. Failure to love the unlovely, to forgive where forgiveness is needed, to share with those who are needy, to care about the victims of crime—all these deny our risen Lord and Savior.

It is significant for us that Jesus called Peter to discipleship twice, early in His ministry and after His resurrection. God commissions and recommissions sinful, imperfect people to accomplish His purpose that all His beloved children be reconciled to Him. And in grace He gives abundant love and forgiveness, and the creative power of His Spirit, so that we can be caring, sharing, committed disciples.

John 21:15-17

How do you show that you really love Jesus? Do you love Him more than the world does?

If it is My will that he remain until I come, what is that to you?
John 21:22

Peter was always impulsive and inquisitive, perpetually questioning Jesus and the disciples about what was going on. He continued to do it with the risen Lord.

102

Peter had just been commissioned by Jesus to carry the message of salvation to the world: "Feed My lambs; tend My sheep." Immediately thereafter Jesus informed Peter as to the cost of his allegiance: He would be crucified as his Lord was. Seeing John, Peter asked Jesus out of sheer curiosity, "Lord, what about this man?" Jesus replied, "If it is My will that he remain until I come, what is that to you? Follow Me!" He was telling Peter quite bluntly that his concern should be only for his own personal mission. What happened to John was of no real consequence to Peter or anyone else. "Follow Me!" spells out in no uncertain terms what that mission was to be—to take up Jesus' work in discipleship after He returned to the Father.

It is destructive to mission to compare one's own special kind of discipleship to that of another. Jealousy and envy, feelings of inadequacy and inferiority, discouragement and failure cause us to lose sight of God's will and purpose for our lives. They also distract us from the truth that God gives us the power and the strength to accomplish His will according to our own calling. They can weaken resolve. What my neighbor does should never influence my task or the urgency with which it must be accomplished.

Each of us is to serve according to our calling. We are not to be concerned with the nature of another's mission. Each individual disciple has a very special task of his own. All are equally precious in the sight of God, yet each one is unique. All are essential to the accomplishment of the enormous task of feeding the Savior's sheep.

John 21:18-23

What is God's will for *your* life? How do you know?

Antagonists to Discipleship in the Kingdom of God

Are grapes gathered from thorns, or figs from thistles?

Matthew 7:16

In the Old Testament, prophets were set apart by their dress. They wore sheepskin garments and were therefore recognized as prophets. When Jesus taught His disciples: "Beware of false prophets, who come to you in sheep's clothing but inwardly are ravenous wolves. You will know them by their fruits," He was warning them against teachers and leaders who would attempt to pervert His Gospel of love and forgiveness under false pretenses. "Wolves" in the Old Testament referred to false prophets or leaders; "wolves" in the New Testament referred to those persons who perverted the truth or persecuted the church. It was a metaphor easily understood by the disciples and the early Christians.

Lest they fail to understand, Jesus continued with a question which had only one clear-cut answer: "Are grapes gathered from thorns, or figs from thistles?" Grapes grow only on grapevines; figs grow only on fig trees!

Paul warned about the same problem in his farewell to the elders at Ephesus: "Take heed to yourselves and to all the flock, in which the Holy Spirit has made you overseers, to care for the church of God which He obtained with the blood of His own Son. I know that after my departure fierce wolves will come in among you, not sparing the flock; and from your own selves will arise men speaking perverse things, to draw away the disciples after them."

The admonitions of Jesus and Paul are as valid today as they were in the first century. Our responsibility as Christians is to witness in gratitude to the saving grace of our Lord and Savior. Our genuineness is demonstrated by what we do, not by what we claim to be. The fruits by which disciples are known are "love, joy, peace, patience, kindness, goodness, faithfulness, gentleness, self-control."

Matthew 7:15-20; Luke 6:43-45; Acts 20:28-31; Galatians 5:16-24

How can you identify and avoid false prophets—within the church, in cults?

But to what shall I compare this generation?

Matthew 11:16

John and Jesus were both rejected by "this generation." They both preached repentance. John was an ascetic, stern and solemn—and was called a demoniac by the crowds. Jesus came enjoying the beauty and loveliness of the world in which He served, and the fellowship and companionship of those whom He came to serve—and He was called a glutton and drunkard.

"To what shall I compare this generation?" Jesus told the crowds a little parable about children's games. The children of Jesus' time often played games about weddings or funerals. The wedding games were full of joy, with dancing and music; but the funeral games were solemn and sad, with much pretense of wailing and mourning. In Jesus' parable, when one group of children wanted to play "wedding"—"we piped to you"—the other group refused to dance. When one group wanted to play "funeral," they "wailed" as did mourners, but the other group refused to "weep." The crowds who came to John were like the children; they were not satisfied with his gloomy predictions of judgment. Neither were the crowds who came to hear Jesus satisfied with Him—the Bridegroom whose message was filled with the joy of the Gospel—love, forgiveness, hope, and eternal life in the kingdom of God.

"Yet wisdom is justified by her deeds," was Jesus' concluding statement. To the Hebrew, wisdom meant God Himself and His divine plan for the reconciliation of all humankind. God did not reject either Jesus or John. He was the Truth who inspired and guided John.

Today there are some who "pipe" but are rejected by those who criticize the liturgy and music because it is too fast or too happy, who find fault with the church's physical plant, who are unhappy with social ministry programs, who feel that benevolence is really unnecessary, who want the pastor to preach moralisms instead of Gospel. But there are many who dance to the piper, who know the peace of forgiveness, who want to share the Gospel, who cannot contain their enthusiasm and joy in serving in God's kingdom. The wedding feast goes on into eternity.

Matthew 11:16-19; Luke 7:31-35

How do you assess our generation as compared to Christ's—in similarities, in differences?

And why do you transgress the commandment of God for the sake of your tradition?

Matthew 15:3

The Pharisees and scribes put their own rules, their tradition, above God's law. They came to Jesus asking why His disciples did not wash their hands before they ate—thus transgressing the tradition of the elders. Jesus retorted with a question of His own: "Why do you transgress the commandment of God for the sake of your tradition?" Hand washing before eating was not done for the sake of hygiene. Rather, it was a symbolic gesture to guarantee ritual purity and cleanness.

Jesus confronted them with an example from their tradition which totally denied God's law. God commanded: "Honor your father and your mother." But according to the oral tradition, if a man dedicated all of his possessions to God and the temple (even though he could still make use of them), he no longer had to support his parents. He was thereby exonerated from obeying God's law. Or if a man made an oath *(corban)* refusing to help his parents, the scribes ruled that the oath could not be broken. Therefore if the man repented and wanted to help his parents, it was forbidden because he dared not break *corban*. Jesus berated them because they were using their tradition to insist that a man break God's law of love and compassion. The spirit of God's written law was in the interpretation of the elders. "This people honors Me with their lips, but their heart is far from Me; in vain do they worship Me, teaching as doctrines the precepts of men."

The Christian church of the first century was embroiled in conflict over these traditions of men. We do not fight that battle today. But we do suffer controversies over matters of worship—the use of varied musical instruments in the liturgical service, the use of paraments and vestments, the hour and length of the service, the participation of lay persons in the Eucharist, the use of individual Communion cups, ordinary bread versus wafers, wedding traditions, tithing, and the placement of the national flag in the church. We dare not allow such disagreements to hide the light and truth of the Gospel, to turn seekers away from worship and the sacraments, and to bury God's gifts of grace under superficial forms and destructive controversy.

Matthew 15:1-9; Mark 7:1-13

How do we transgress the commandments of God by human traditions?

Are you also still without understanding? Do you not see that whatever goes into the mouth passes into the stomach, and so passes on?

Matthew 15:16-17

With a short saying of great impact Jesus continued His discourse against the tradition of the elders: "Hear and understand: not what goes into the mouth defiles a man, but what comes out of the mouth, this defiles a man." But they did not understand. Peter asked Jesus for an explanation.

The extreme dietary and cleansing demands of the rabbinic tradition were no longer valid; in fact, they never had been. They were absolutely irrelevant to Jesus' Gospel. Many times the traditions of past generations can be erased only with great difficulty—they can become stumbling blocks to important new concepts.

Jesus' explanation is as simple as was the short saying: "Do you not see that whatever goes into the mouth passes into the stomach, and so passes on? But what comes out of the mouth proceeds from the heart, and this defiles a man." It is one's heart and not one's hands that needs to be cleansed.

The words which come out of our mouth, which is only the vehicle to transport them, express the deepest feelings and longings of the heart and the innermost thoughts and reasonings of the mind. They can be good words of understanding, compassion, forgiveness, and healing. But they can be evil and scornful words, and those are what defile. "For out of the heart come evil thoughts, murder, adultery, fornication, theft, false witness, slander."

Discipleship is expressed by words and feelings as well as deeds and conduct. All the so-called "good works" in the world cannot save us. Actually, they can be antagonists to discipleship, for it is easy to convince oneself that outward displays of piety are acceptable to God. Tithing and contributions to church and community are meaningless if the heart is unclean—if it does not know or share love. "If I give away all I have, and if I deliver my body to be burned, but have not love, I gain nothing."

But from the heart that knows forgiveness comes love which is "patient and kind ... not jealous or boastful ... not arrogant or rude ... does not insist on its own way ... is not irritable or resentful ... does not rejoice at wrong, but rejoices in the right."

Matthew 15:10-20; Mark 7:14-23; 1 Corinthians 13:1-7

Do you understand Jesus' question sufficiently to discard impediments and contradictions to the Gospel and Christian freedom?

When therefore the owner of the vineyard comes, what will he do to those tenants?
Matthew 21:40

The parable of the vineyard, addressed to the chief priests and Pharisees, speaks of our relationship to God in His kingdom.

The owner who planted the vineyard was God. He gave His tenants everything they needed to produce an abundant crop of fruit. The tenants were the entire Israelite nation. Theirs was the responsibility of sharing God's Gospel of love and grace—the fruit of repentance, reconciliation, righteousness, and harmony with God. The servants whom the owner sent to the tenants were the prophets, who time after time begged, implored, exhorted, reproached, and admonished the Israelites to repent, to return to their God. He would abundantly pardon! The son whom the tenants rejected and killed was Jesus.

One can discern in this simple parable the profound depths of God's infinite grace. He gave us everything—His magnificent creation; His very self in the incarnation, life, death, and resurrection of His only beloved Son; His Spirit of truth who creates faith, leads us to repentance, and forgives us over and over again, every day of our lives. He stoops to us constantly; He never stops seeking us. But He never forces us to conform; He gave us the freedom to reject His offer of reconciliation. When we respond to the bidding of His Spirit, we are the servants. When we reject the bidding of His Spirit, we are the tenants.

Self-serving and pride got in the way of the tenants; they wanted what rightly belonged to the owner. They deliberately disobeyed and rebelled against God.

"When therefore the owner . . . comes, what will he do to those tenants?" The kingdom of God will be taken away and given to a nation which will produce the fruits of righteousness. A nation without state or national boundaries, distinctions of race or social class, political or ideological divisions—that will be the vineyard of our loving God, the Christian church. It is a church where each one becomes a new creation in Baptism, where one's sinful self will "be drowned and die with all sins and evil lusts" through daily repentance, and where day after day a new self will arise to "live before God in righteousness and purity forever" (Luther's Small Catechism).

Matthew 21:33-48; Mark 12:1-12; Luke 20:9-19

What kind of fruit does God have a right to expect from us? How much are we giving Him? How willingly?

For which is greater, the gold or the temple that has made the gold sacred? . . . For which is greater, the gift or the altar that makes the gift sacred?

Matthew 23:17, 19

Among the ordinary people of Palestine oath-taking was a very common practice in everyday life. An oath was a solemn pledge or promise that a person's word was true and that he intended to carry out what he promised. The purpose of the oath was to bind the one who took the oath to his promise. The rabbis tried to discourage oath-taking, but if a person insisted on taking an oath, he had to follow the proper form. The legalists also had a series of rules designed to help that same person evade his oath. The only really binding oaths were those made in the name of God; they absolutely had to be kept.

Jesus' question is addressed to the irrational and illogical practice of oath-taking. It is also an attack on the doctors of the law who supported such practices and who, furthermore, devised means for evading the oath, which encouraged people to break their promises and to deny the integrity of their word.

111

Some rabbis taught that certain kinds of oaths taken by the temple or altar were binding only if they were taken by the gold of the altar or the gift that was on the altar. Jesus tore away this ridiculous pretense by arguing that he who swears by the altar swears by everything on the altar and by God who is worshiped at the altar, that he who swears by the temple swears by it and by God who dwells in the temple. Therefore no man-made rules apply; the oaths are binding since they are made in the presence of God and thereby sworn by God.

Today one is required to take an oath—to promise to tell the whole truth and nothing but the truth—in a court of law. That is a requirement of our judicial system, a civil matter which is not bound to religious law as it was in Jesus' time.

Our integrity and honesty should never have to be affirmed by swearing or oath-taking where our relationship to fellow persons is concerned. To swear by God today is as foolish and sinful as it was then. God knows what is in our hearts; He hears what we say. It is better simply to say "Yes" or "No" and avoid unnecessary oaths.

Matthew 23:16-22

What oaths does God expect us to make to Him? What is wrong with oath-taking in human matters?

Why does this generation seek a sign?
Mark 8:12

Many of the Pharisees were continually hostile to Jesus' ministry. They demanded "a sign from heaven" in order to test Him. They had witnessed a variety of miracles and signs but were still blind to these evidences of Jesus' Messiahship. Now they wanted some spectacular display from the heavens—a brilliant flash of blinding light, an impressive display of lightening bolts, or a roaring crash of thunder.

Jesus answered the Pharisee's demands in disgust: "Why does this generation seek a sign? Truly, I say to you, no sign shall be given to this generation." He must have become increasingly impatient with their unbelief.

"Generation" here means a particular group of people, the

Pharisees. It can also have apocalyptic portent—all generations before that time and since have been faithless and perverse. The Israelites in the wilderness constantly demanded proofs of God's power and goodwill, even though He had delivered them from slavery and continually sustained them.

There are Christians today who seek signs—speaking in tongues, prophesying, healing. They fail to see God's power in the magnificent beauty of creation. They fail to feel God's power and love in the "peace that passes all understanding." They fail to sense God's Spirit in the growth of one's faith and commitment. They want more, and yet there is no more impressive, spectacular, moving proof than the sign of Jonah—the resurrection of our Lord and Savior Jesus Christ.

We need no additional signs to warn us that the end is coming—it is as close to us as our own death. Never must we allow so-called signs to deter us from the truth about God's infinite grace and love, or from our mission in discipleship. Rather we must be about our Father's business and be ready for His coming at any time.

We have the record of the Bible; the countless promises of God; the life, death, and resurrection of His Son; the witness of countless saints over the years despite persecution, violence, and even death; the expressions of faith in our weekly worship; and the day-by-day commitment of our fellow Christians—what more do we need?

Mark 8:11-13; Matthew 12:38-42; Luke 11:29-32

Why is Christ's resurrection our final, all-conclusive sign?

Is it not written, "My house shall be called a house of prayer for all the nations"?
Mark 11:17

The temple in Jerusalem ("My house") during Jesus' time was the temple which Herod had restored after the exile. On the lower level of the temple area was the court of the Gentiles, where both Jew and Gentile were allowed. This was also the court where those who failed to pay their annual temple tax in their villages in March had to come to fulfill that obligation, where money changers operated their booths, and where merchants sold sacrificial animals or doves to the

113

pilgrims who came to offer sacrifices during the Passover celebration.

According to Jewish law the temple tax could be paid only with half-shekel coins; foreign coins were considered unclean. Therefore all the pilgrims from outside of Palestine had to change their coins, as did those from Palestine who had larger coins than the half-shekel. That of itself should have caused no difficulty, but the money changers often charged exorbitant rates. The temple treasury grew fat at the expense of those who could least afford to pay. It was a gross display of social injustice. These same pilgrims were forced to buy sacrificial animals or doves inside the court of the Gentiles at much higher prices than those purchased outside of the temple, which inspectors could declare ritually unclean and therefore unfit for sacrifice.

Gentiles were permitted only in this court. There were signs posted along the law wall separating the court of the Gentiles from the rest of the temple warning that any Gentile who went beyond would be killed. Lost sight of, apparently, was the universality of the Abrahamic covenant of grace: "I will bless you . . . so that you will be a blessing. . . . In you all the families of the earth shall be blessed" (Genesis 12:1-3).

Jesus' question: "Is it not written, 'My house shall be called a house of prayer for all the nations'?" is an angry condemnation of those who practiced exploitation and yet believed that by displaying the outward form of their religion, particularly in ceremonial and sacrifical worship, they were carrying out God's will. It was also a plea for the proclamation of the Gospel to all nations and races without prejudice.

Mark 11:15-17; Matthew 21:12-13; Luke 19:45-46; John 2:13-17

How might we allow greed and prejudice to get in the way of mission?

Man, who made Me a judge or divider over you?
Luke 12:14

According to Jewish tradition, if any person had a dispute with someone else, he consulted a rabbi. The rabbi was highly trained. He had to be proficient in ecclesiastical, ceremonial, moral, and civil law.

114

He had to be an expert in the interpretation of Scripture.

Perhaps because he believed Jesus to be a rabbi or because he was impressed with Jesus' knowledge of the Scriptures, a man came to Him with a problem concerning an inheritance. Jesus refused to act the role of judge—that belonged to the governing agents of Caesar. Jesus was concerned with spiritual relationships within the kingdom of God. "Take heed," He said, "and beware of all covetousness; for a man's life does not consist in the abundance of his possessions." To further clarify His refusal, Jesus told the parable of the rich fool.

A rich man had land which produced so bountifully that he had no place to store his crops. So he tore down his barns and built much bigger ones to accommodate his riches. Satisfied with himself, he said, "Soul, you have ample goods laid up for many years; take your ease, eat, drink, be merry." But that night he died.

All the material wealth in the world is meaningless if one is not reconciled to God. The poor rich fool never looked beyond his physical life—he was completely self-centered. He might consider his relationship to God sometime in the future, he thought, but now it could be postponed. His goal was only to satisfy himself instantly, here and now—retire, eat, drink, be merry. His was a false security.

The only true security on our threatened planet is to be found when we are in harmony with God's purpose for our lives and the lives of all the other inhabitants of the earth. For then, out of the abundance of the heart, grateful for the peace of reconciliation, flows the desire to share both spiritual and material wealth.

Luke 12:13-21; Matthew 6:19-21

How do you see the materialism of our age interfering with discipleship?

Did I not choose you, the twelve, and one of you is a devil?
John 6:70

None of us can take our spiritual relationship to God for granted. This is what Jesus implied in His question which followed Peter's confession of faith: "You have the words of eternal life; and we have

115

believed, and have come to know, that You are the Holy One of God."
Peter was speaking for the Twelve just after many of Jesus' other
followers had abandoned Him.

To be called by Jesus, to be one of His 12 closest disciples, to be
with Him during the three years of His ministry, did not guarantee
unwavering faith and loyalty. Judas betrayed his Lord and Savior; the
11 disciples "forsook Him and fled" after Judas came to the garden
with a great crowd, and Peter denied that he had even known his
Master.

We are no different than the Twelve. We were created with the
freedom to reject God's gracious love and forgiveness, to refuse His
call to discipleship, to yield to the temptation of Satan to "be like
God." Satan does not force us to believe his cunning lies; he simply
caters to the "old Adam" in each of us who would like to control his
own destiny, independent of God.

"Did I not choose you . . . and one of you is a devil?" is addressed
to all of us as a warning against being a disciple in name only. Jesus
calls and chooses us in Baptism. He requires full commitment. There
is no middle ground: "He who is not with Me is against Me, and he who
does not gather with Me scatters" (Matthew 12:30). The devils Jesus
was talking about are those who do not yield to the pleading of the
Spirit to repent. For those who repent, God's forgiveness is always
available. They enter into a close relationship with their Lord, being
members of His body, the church, where "He daily and richly forgives
all sins to me and all believers" (Luther's Small Catechism).

John 6:66-71

How can a disciple (follower) of Christ become a devil (a destroyer of
Christ's work)? What guarantee do we have that we will not be guilty
of apostasy?

Why do you not understand what I say? . . . Which of you convicts Me of sin? If I tell the truth, why do you not believe Me?
John 8:43, 46

Jesus' question was a terrible indictment of His unbelieving
countrymen. "Why do you not understand what I say? It is because

116

you cannot bear to hear My word. You are of your father the devil, and your will is to do your father's desires. . . . Which of you convicts Me of sin?" It was terrible because the Son of God was condemning their rejection of Him and, consequently, of God who had sent Him to them. It was terrible because Jesus bluntly accused them of following Satan.

His countrymen, however, failed to understand Jesus' words. They insisted that they were the children of Abraham, that God was their Father. But Jesus denied their claim. The children of Abraham are those who trust in the Messiah promised as the Seed of Abraham.

The covenant of grace which God made with Abraham—"Look toward heaven, and number the stars, if you are able to number them. . . . So shall your descendants be" (Genesis 15:5)—was never intended to be confined only to the physical descendants of Abraham. It was to encompass a spiritual family "from every nation, from all tribes and peoples and tongues" (Revelation 7:9)—the kingdom of God. Israel was to be the vehicle through which the covenant would move over the centuries until the time when God would send His Son to reconcile the world to Himself.

Jesus' question is a terrible indictment of unbelief in the world today. The Gospel has gone out far and wide. Our sinless Christ—"the Way, the Truth, and the Life"—is not responsible for unbelief. It comes from something inherent in human nature—pride, the reluctance to give up sinful ways, idolatrous materialism, etc. Why are these forces so strong? Because the power of evil, Satan, appeals to the flesh. Because surrender to the will of God is not widely practiced, even within the church. "If I tell the truth, why do you not believe Me?" And believing—worship and serve Him?

John 8:39-47

Why would anyone today *not* believe in Christ, considering all the evidences of His Messiahship?

Do you now believe?
John 16:31

It was almost too late—just hours before Jesus went to the Garden of Gethsemane for the last time to pray. Judas had already left to do his evil work of betrayal. After three years of constant companionship, innumerable hours of private dialog and public teaching, and countless healings and miracles, the 11 disciples finally acknowledged that Jesus had come from God: "Ah, now You are speaking plainly, not in any figure! Now we know that You know all things, and need none to question You; by this we believe You came from God."

We are aware that in several instances of healing and "signs" Jesus asked that He not be publicly declared to be the Messiah. But these were His dearest, most intimate friends. Jesus must have experienced deep sadness when He asked the question: "Do you now believe?" for He followed it with a poignant corroboration of a prophecy from the sacred Scriptures.

Many, many years before, a young man returned to Jerusalem from captivity in Babylon. He was Zechariah, called by God to be His prophet, who declared: "Strike the shepherd, that the sheep may be scattered" (Zechariah 13:7). Jesus reminded His 11 beloved disciples of that prophecy: "You will be scattered, every man to his home, and will leave Me alone; yet I am not alone, for the Father is with Me." Soon the disciples would be faced with much sorrow and testing, tribulation and suffering. But as always, Jesus' compassion and love tempered the prophecy with a promise of grace: "In Me you . . . have peace. . . . I have overcome the world."

Jesus knew His disciples well; He also knows each one of us. He knows our strengths and weaknesses, our ability to face the challenges of the world and Satan, our victories and our failures. He knows that we too will face testing, and He gives us the courage and strength, wisdom and understanding—the armor to fight off the temptations of the world and the wiley cajoling of the Tempter.

It is never too late to believe. Jesus has a superabundance of love and forgiveness. All we need do is accept that love and allow the Holy Spirit to work in our lives. And, like Jesus, we are never alone. The Father is with us through the redemptive love of the Son and the counseling of His Spirit.

John 16:29-33

Do you now believe? Why?

So, could you not watch with Me one hour? . . .
Are you still sleeping and taking your rest?

Matthew 26:40, 45

Jesus' tortured agony in the Garden of Gethsemane was compounded by the disobedience, inattention, and lethargy of the disciples, especially the three He chose to accompany Him to "watch with Me." But after the emotionally taxing experiences in the upper room they were far more concerned with the need for rest and sleep. Therefore Jesus wrestled alone: "My Father, if it be possible, let this cup pass from Me; nevertheless, not as I will, but as Thou wilt." Intense inner suffering caused by the weight of the world's sins and by the anticipation of what He knew would be the cruel suffering of the cross engulfed Him for a little time—sorrow which was almost worse than death. But Jesus' agonized prayer ended in acceptance, triumph over the temptation to turn aside from His appointed course. He chose to obey the will of the Father.

It was not so with the disciples. Even Jesus' admonition to them when He found them sleeping, "Watch and pray that you may not enter into temptation; the spirit indeed is willing, but the flesh is weak," did not fully rouse them. They failed to honor Jesus' request to "watch with Me." Flesh proved stronger than spirit.

It is absolutely essential today that Christians "watch and pray." Temptations are so subtle and beguiling, catering to one's spiritual and physical weaknesses. It is only through God's Word that we observe our Savior's agony as He pays the price of our redemption. We will never experience a situation even remotely like that of the disciples. But there is a lesson to learn as we follow Jesus.

Could you not devote just one short hour a week to worship? Could you not stay awake for one comparatively short sermon? Could you not attend Bible study for one short hour? Could you not find time to visit a sick or bereaved friend in your busy schedule? Could you not examine yourself—your spiritual condition—objectively for just one hour?

God commands us to share ourselves as Jesus did. Can we do it? Indeed we can! God followed His command with His gifts of Word and sacrament and Spirit! We can do God's will because we have the greatest help in the world.

Matthew 26:36-46; Mark 14:32-42; Luke 22:39-46

What kind of incentive would cause you to rearrange your life and your busy days in order to do the will of the Father? What would you have to change in your life and timetable to share yourself in commitment and discipleship?

Friend, why are you here?
Matthew 26:50

Jesus' straightforward question, addressed to Judas, "Friend, why are you here?" is filled to overflowing with *grace*. All that is God's grace and steadfast love is expressed in those five plain little words. Grace is such a deceptively simple word, but it embodies the holiness and majesty of our living God who freely offers all of us His steadfast love by involving Himself in our lives even though we might rebel—and even when we do. He involves Himself in our lives because He is always—forever—reaching out, seeking us, offering forgiveness over and over and over again, and constantly cultivating and strengthening our relationship to Him.

And in that beautiful word "friend" is embodied the essence of righteousness. As Friend, Jesus brought the Gospel and the kingdom of God to the poor, the tax-collectors and sinners—all of us. As Friend, He showed us how much He loved us by dying for us. In fact, while we were still His enemies, He laid down His life for us. As Friend, He frees us from bondage to ourselves so that we can serve others as friends. Jesus was our example of true friendship. He willingly and consciously devoted Himself to the reconciliation of all whom He calls friend.

That same grace was offered to Judas, who Jesus knew had betrayed Him—forgiveness offered freely to one who had sinned. But Judas knew no repentance then. He was still blinded by his greed. He could not be a friend to Jesus.

Christian friendship cannot be discriminatory. The friendship of Jesus is connected with concern for the freedom and dignity of all persons, everywhere. Jesus provides the perfect model of friendship. His friendship for us calls for a response in kind: loyalty, love, and cheerful service.

120

Matthew 26:47-50; Luke 22:47-48; John 15:12-17

What is it about Christ that convinces you that He is your Friend?
What about you ought to convince you that you are His friend?

The Cost
of
Discipleship
in the
Kingdom of God

Are not two sparrows sold for a penny?
Matthew 10:29

Jesus' teaching is filled with contrasts, picturesque in their simplicity yet filled with impressive revelations of grace. The tiny sparrow—the poor man's meat, the cheapest thing he could buy—is never forgotten by God; He knows its every movement as it flies through the air and lights on the ground. But human beings, created in the image of God, are infinitely more valuable than many, many sparrows. "Even the hairs of your head are all numbered."

"What is man that Thou art mindful of him, and the son of man that Thou dost care for him? Yet thou hast made him little less than God, and dost crown him with glory and honor."

It is each one's "glory and honor" to share the Gospel of grace—of God's love, mercy, and forgiveness in Christ. God insists on obedience to His will and purpose for all humanity. That is the meaning of discipleship. The responsibility of discipleship is to offer God's reconciling gifts of grace by proclaiming Jesus as Savior and Lord.

Jesus warned His disciples that the cost of discipleship would be extremly high. As He Himself did, they would face persecution and even death for boldly proclaiming the Gospel. But proclaim it they must! They were to be witnesses to the "ends of the earth" after He left them. "Do not fear those who kill the body but cannot kill the soul; rather fear Him who can destroy both soul and body in hell."

To fear God is not the same as fearing men. To fear men is to be aware that persons who are not in harmony with God's purpose for their life have the capability of destroying one's mission in discipleship—even to the extent of inflicting bodily harm or death. But to fear God is to recognize the divinity of God, His sovereignty over heaven and earth—from the tiny, insignificant sparrow to man, who is "little less than God," or "a little lower than the angels" (KJV). It is to recognize the seriousness of His commandments, the earnestness of His love, and the urgency of bringing His grace to a dying humanity.

Matthew 10:26-33; Luke 12:2-9; Psalm 8:4-5
What kinds of events or cultural changes do you perceive to be a threat to the Christian's mission today—ethical, moral, religious, or psychological?

For what will it profit a man, if he gains the whole world and forfeits his life? Or what shall a man give in return for his life?

Matthew 16:26

Everywhere one looks, statements are being made about the value of life. Television takes us almost instantly to all parts of our planet—to witness natural and manmade disasters. We can see, hear, and feel the consequences of hurricanes, tornadoes, earthquakes, conflagrations, and wars.

The loss of property alone is difficult to comprehend. But the greatest tragedy is the loss of even a single life. And if physical life is so priceless, how much more valuable is life in the everlasting kingdom of God?

The life of this age and of that which is to come are inseparably tied together. The only real and worthwhile life is that which is a part of the kingdom of God—here and in eternity. That life can be experienced only through faith in what God has done for us in creation, redemption, and sanctification, through trust in God's infinite mercy, and in selfless obedience to His will. It is the costly life of discipleship in which the one who serves is released from self-service to living the Christ-life.

Possessions, the power of wealth and authority, and the pride of ambition eventually become worthless if faith and humble dependence on God's mercy are sacrificed in climbing the ladder of worldly success. When one forfeits faith and trust in God in favor of self-reliance, it becomes easier and easier to rationalize practices which are morally and ethically wrong. In the relentless pursuit of possessions the only real life is lost—the life which continues after death. "For the Son of Man is to come with His angels in the glory of His Father, and then He will repay every man for what he has done."

But to those who follow the costly road of discipleship in selfless service—so often accompanied by rejection, derision, scorn, loneliness, and persecution—the King will say: "Come, O blessed of My Father, inherit the kingdom prepared for you from the foundation of the world; for I was hungry and you gave Me food, I was thirsty and you gave Me drink, I was a stranger and you welcomed Me, I was naked and you clothed Me, I was sick and you visited Me, I was in prison and you came to Me" (Matthew 25:34-36).

Matthew 16:24-28; Mark 8:34-37; Luke 9:23-27

How can you explain the greed and lust for power which are so destructive to families, communities, nations, and the entire world?

Do you think that I have come to give peace on earth?

Luke 12:51

The Jews believed that when the Messiah came He would bring them peace—freedom from aggression, war, and violence. But the peace He promised them, and for which He came, was not an earthly peace but spiritual peace—*shalom*. It was the peace of grace—forgiveness and reconciliation—harmony with God, with oneself, with one's fellow persons, and with the creation—all the product of the Prince of Peace.

Therefore this question Jesus asked His disciples is a paradox. I can have the "peace . . . which passes all understanding," inner tranquillity and deep, abiding faith, while at the same time I am unhappy and sad over personal relationships, family dissensions, racial violence, the predicament of the aged in inflation and recession, the daily reports in the media of beatings, rapes, and murder, and the exploitation of the creation. I am also aware that the stand I take in response to my faith can cause divisions—even within the family.

Jesus' question and His reply were an offense to His countrymen. It was a radical concept, contrary to the high esteem in which they held close family relationships. But Jesus' reasoning was sound. Certainly it is in evidence today, everywhere we look. Family attachments can get in the way of Christian commitment. Deep rifts occur between parents and children, young people and the elderly, over the interpretation of Biblical concepts and the expression of faith. Piety gets all mixed up with morals and culture. Consequently the real meaning of God's will that every person be saved is lost in the conflict. In Japan, as well as in our own country, confessing Christians are rejected and ostracized by their families. The cost of discipleship can be very great—heartbreak, sorrow, loneliness, and unhappiness.

But those who are in harmony with God, and therefore know the "peace . . . which passes all understanding," are able to bear in faith the heartbreak of divisions within their own families and the family of the church. By loving example and with kindness, patience, prayer, and sacrifice they continue to reach out in compassion to all whom Christ has redeemed. God never stops loving and seeking. Nor do His children.

Luke 12:49-53; Philippians 4:7

Examine the relationships of those around you? Is there peace on earth? What can you do to bring it about?

Which of you, desiring to build a tower, does not first sit down and count the cost, whether he has enough to complete it? . . . Or what king, going to encounter another king in war, will not sit down first and take counsel whether he is able with ten thousand to meet him who comes against him with twenty thousand?

Luke 14:28, 31

Jesus was followed by "multitudes" who anticipated a victorious political empire when He reached Jersualem. To temper their enthusiasm for a kingdom which would never exist, Jesus told them two parables designed to make them think long and hard about the cost of following Him.

The first parable was about building. No conscientious builder ever digs a foundation before he carefully surveys the entire project from beginning to end to see whether he has enough money and supplies to complete it. If he does not initially count the cost, he may not be able to finish his structure. He would then be subject to ridicule. The American West today is filled with many such projects which failed. Bankrupt families and businesses, ghost towns, and irreparably damaged land—the failures remain to remind us that defeat cannot be hidden.

The second parable concerns a wise king who will not go into battle against enormous odds without first consulting his trusted advisers and seeking peace. We have observed disasters in the Mid-East and elsewhere in the last several years because leaders failed to count the cost of war. Their defeats have embroiled many nations in turmoil and uncertainty.

Jesus is warning us today: Do not take the responsibility of discipleship lightly. It is the greatest calling that anyone can have. But the cost must be weighed carefully lest we fail.

The call to discipleship should not be accepted during an emotional high—emotional decisions are often spur of the moment and short-lived. Nor should it be accepted when one is in trouble and despair; when things change and the situation is reversed, the role of discipleship is often forgotten. A too easily made commitment may become failure when the road becomes rough.

One can count the cost of discipleship realistically, knowing one will face many of the adversities Jesus did—but also knowing that a person need not fail. Jesus has already been on the same road which we follow—and because He did not consider His sacrifice too costly, He was able to send us the Holy Spirit to guide, protect, counsel, and encourage. Do not give up!

Luke 14:25-33; Matthew 10:37-38

Have you experienced the high cost of discipleship? Would you consider it too high, especially when seen in the light of eternity?

Who is My mother, and who are My brothers?
Matthew 12:48

Jesus was teaching and healing in Capernaum. Great crowds came to hear Him from all of Galilee and beyond. There were doctors of the Law who came down from Jerusalem to hear Him and to "test" Him. Many of the people saw Him only as a miracle worker and an exorcist. They failed to understand that the Son of God was working out God's plan of salvation among them.

Jesus' mother and brothers came from Nazareth to Capernaum to the home where He was staying, asking to see Him. Why? We do not know. Matthew gives no reason; Mark implies that they were concerned about His well-being.

Family ties were deeply treasured among the Jews. The teaching of the Law was a responsibility of the head of the family. The Passover was celebrated in the home. The family was bound together by religious and spiritual concerns as well as kinship. It is this close familial and spiritual unity which has kept Judaism alive.

By His question Jesus was not rejecting or denying His family. Rather, He was making it clear that in His kingdom spiritual ties are more binding than family ties. One's spiritual family is to be of greater importance than one's natural family. Jesus' true or real family consisted of His disciples—spiritual Israel, the Church—whose common bond was obedience to God's will. "Whoever does the will of My Father in heaven is My brother, and sister, and mother."

There is also deep pathos in Jesus' question. Many Christians from the time of the early church until today have experienced ridicule, derision, rejection, or ostracism by relatives who refuse to recognize God and His disciples. Jesus' own family did not perceive that He was God's own Son. He understands.

For many Christians throughout the world, the church is their true family. For some it is their only family. Because we recognize this to be true, we must show love and concern for each individual member of our local congregations—as well as the masses of people the church serves on our planet.

The kingdom of God is more than a statement of words. It is the fellowship of all disciples who do God's will, whose primary concern is to love their God with all their heart and soul and mind and strength, and to love their neighbor as themselves.

Matthew 12:46-50; Mark 3:31-35

Do you see your congregation as a family? If not, why?

Will you lay down your life for Me?

John 13:38

The time of Jesus' passion and crucifixion was imminent. He was sharing His last supper with His 12 disciples. He had washed their feet in love and humility. He had said to Judas, "What you are going to do, do quickly" (John 13:27). He had told Peter, "Where I am going you cannot follow Me now." Brashly Peter answered, "Lord, why cannot I follow You now? I will lay down my life for You." Jesus' answer, "Will you?" is filled with intense and poignant feeling, for He knew that Peter would deny Him.

All during the history of the Christian Church there have been martyrs who have given their lives for their faith—John the Baptist, Peter, John Hus, and countless missionaries. Some were put to death by enemies of the church, and some—for instance, during the time of the Inquisition—by the church itself. But none of them came to earth willingly and knowingly to die for the sins of humankind as Jesus did. Because He was God, Jesus' entire life and death were self-sacrificial. He "emptied Himself" to show us what God's love was all about.

"Will you lay down your life for Me?" That question requires deep soul-searching. Can we love so much that we would willingly, voluntarily go to Jerusalem, knowing that humiliation, scourging, and crucifixion lay at the end of the road?

The love of God for His creatures is beyond human comprehension. Because Jesus was (and is) God, it is impossible to compare martyrdom, or the father or mother who risks life to save a child, or the stranger who endangers himself to help someone drowning or caught in a burning building, to God's supreme sacrifice. His is an act of inexpressible, ineffable divine love. It is impossible to compare the premeditated, voluntary self-sacrifice of Jesus to any human act—even though it may result in death.

There are risks and costs in discipleship. As much as we claim to love our God and our fellow persons, there is always the possibility that we too, like Peter, will deny our Lord. There is no way of knowing just how we would respond in the face of certain death.

"Greater love has no man than this, that a man lay down his life for his friends. You are My friends if you do what I command you" (John 15:13-14).

John 13:36-38; Matthew 26:33-35; Mark 14:29-31; Luke 22:31-34

Do you know of any instances where a person willingly went to his death for the sake of another? Is the possibility of martyrdom included in your concept of loyalty to Christ?

Are you able to drink the cup that I drink, or to be baptized with the baptism with which I am baptized?

Mark 10:38

Jesus and His disciples were on the way to Jerusalem, Jesus willingly going to what He knew was to be suffering and death. In vivid and stark language—"mock, spit, scourge, kill"—He told them what awaited Him. They were bewildered and afraid. But they did not understand.

For many of Jesus' contemporaries the hope of the kingdom of God was in an earthly kingdom like David's or Solomon's. It was to be a kingdom of glory. A suffering king was entirely alien to their hopes and desires.

James and John were much like you and me—it is very difficult for any of us to be completely free of personal ambition. They believed they were following a man who would be a king. Their request to be put in positions of power and honor in His kingdom was very human.

Jesus' question to them, in which He again refers to His passion and crucifixion (cup and baptism here mean suffering) failed to intimidate them. They did not lose faith in Jesus. They were willing to suffer with Him in order to bring about His kingdom.

In the kingdom of God it is God alone who bestows grace and favor, forgiveness and reconciliation. He makes no distinctions on the basis of culture, social status, or economic privilege. No one earns or sacrifices his way into that kingdom. None of the faithful are promised a position of power of distinction.

Those who serve in His kingdom must follow the way of the cross. And greatness in such a kingdom becomes service to all people. We arrive at the kingdom of glory via the kingdom of suffering.

Mark 10:32-45

How do you perceive suffering in the kingdom of God? How are we "baptized" with our Lord's "baptism"?

When I sent you out with no purse or bag or sandals, did you lack anything?

Luke 22:35

The Scriptures were about to be fulfilled. In the upper room with His disciples Jesus tried to make them understand what was going to happen to Him and to them as well. Deeply saddened, Jesus had just told Peter that he would deny Him three times.

Jesus asked a thoughtful question: "When I sent you out with no purse or bag or sandals, did you lack anything?" During their Galilean ministry they needed no purse or bag or sandals. Jesus and His disciples were generally treated with kindness and hospitality. All their needs were taken care of by the people to whom they ministered. But now there would be a drastic change. The people with whom they mingled in Jerusalem would turn against them! They would face antagonism and persecution in their attempts to evangelize. Therefore Jesus advised them to take their purses and bags—to be prepared for an abrupt and radical reversal of attitude among the people. Hospitality would be denied them; each man would have to fend for himself. It is an agonized and lonely Jesus reaching out to His disciples.

"Let him who has no sword sell his mantle and buy one" is an allegory which Jesus may have used to comfort His friends. In Ephesians 6:17 Paul refers to "the helmet of salvation and the sword of the Spirit, which is the Word of God." Jesus often used allegories in an attempt to explain His admonitions. At any rate, the disciples misunderstood; they thought He meant real swords. Jesus must have despaired at their lack of comprehension. They failed to perceive that even after He left them they would lack nothing.

We, too, lack nothing. We have the sword of the Spirit, the Word of God, at our disposal. And we have the testimony of those brave men and women who through the centuries faced death and persecution to bring it down to us in the church today.

The church has survived almost 2000 years—years of growth as well as persecution. It will continue to spread, perhaps more slowly than we like—but continue it will, because of the disciples today who, having their Lord, fearlessly proclaim the Gospel, lacking nothing.

Luke 22:35-38

Can you boldly proclaim God's love and grace in all your contacts throughout the week in the secure knowledge that you lack nothing?

My God, My God, why hast Thou forsaken Me?

Matthew 27:46

There are times when we are so overwhelmed with awe and thanksgiving for the inexpressible love of God that we forget He is also a God of judgment.

Jesus' whole life was self-offering. The cross was the climax of a life totally dedicated to doing the will of His Father. It is impossible for the human mind to grasp the depth of a love like that of our God of grace. He sent His only Son to live and die. Willingly, out of sheer love for fallen humanity, He faced the agonizing, humiliating, tortured death of crucifixion—the sacrifice of the appointed Lamb of God for the sins of the world.

Jesus' words from the intense physical suffering of the cross, "Father, forgive them; for they know not what they do," and His offer of forgiveness to the repentant criminal, "Truly, I say to you, today you will be with Me in paradise," bear witness to God's unutterable and steadfast love. By contrast, the words, "My God, My God, why hast Thou forsaken Me?" bear witness to the despair and hopelessness of separation from God suffered by the damned in hell. Those words are a cry of terrible loneliness—a cry from One who clung to His loving Father and therefore never gave up trusting!

The final cry of Jesus, "It is finished!" is a cry of triumph. In His self-offering in living and dying, Jesus once and for all time perfectly obeyed God's will for us and fully atoned for our sins. Satan, sin, and spiritual death were defeated for us. We were given the gift of eternal life in the kingdom of God—physical death is nothing to fear! We live in the promise and hope of the resurrection, no longer slave to self and law.

Alienation, abandonment, separation from God never come from God. Any punishment for sin—one's arrogance in putting one's own will before that of God—is the natural result of willfully rejecting

133

God's love and therefore living a sinful life.

Because Christ was forsaken, God never forsakes us! We have the guarantee of the Spirit, who keeps us with Jesus Christ in the one true faith. " 'I will never fail you nor forsake you.' Hence we can confidently say, 'The Lord is my helper, I will not be afraid; what can man do to me?' " (Hebrews 13:5b, 6). We have the promise of Jesus Himself, "Lo, I am with you always, to the close of the age" (Matthew 28:20b). God always keeps His promises! We can be sure of that!

Matthew 27:35-50

Do you know of any instance when you felt God had forsaken you? What made you think so?

Judgment
in the
Kingdom of God

And you, Capernaum, will you be exalted to heaven?

Matthew 11:23

When Jesus first sent out the Twelve to proclaim the kingdom of God, to preach and to heal, He told them what to do in case they met opposition: "Shake off the dust from your feet as you leave that house or town." To reject the disciples was to reject Jesus: "Truly, I say to you, it shall be more tolerable on the day of judgment for the land of Sodom and Gomorrah than for that town."

Now Jesus Himself extended that same warning of judgment to the cities in which He preached and healed. He had gone through the cities of Galilee doing His mighty works—preaching: "The time is fulfilled, and the kingdom of God is at hand; repent, and believe in the Gospel" (Mark 1:15), and performing miracles, evidence and signs of that proclamation. But they had rejected Him.

Jesus warned those cities that their judgment would be worse than that of Tyre and Sidon, Sodom and Gommorrah—for in rejecting Him they rejected the Father. Tyre and Sidon were wicked cities, proud and impenitent; Sodom and Gomorrah were cities filled with depravity and just as unrepentant. But it would be easier for them at the Last Judgment because they had not seen the "mighty works" of Jesus. If they had, they would have repented "in sackcloth and ashes," symbols of the awareness of sin and guilt, of repentance and mourning.

By preferring their nationalistic ambitions to the kingdom of God they were courting political disaster—the imminent destruction of Israel, Jerusalem, and the temple by the Romans—as well as the judgment of God. Capernaum would be "brought down to Hades."

Judgment is real also today. Those who try to act like God, who believe they have their destiny in their own hands, who refuse to perceive that they sin against God and their brothers and sisters, and who refuse to repent will, as surely as Capernaum, face God's awful wrath and judgment. Those who see grace as all sweetness and light and refuse to accept grace's responsibility—their individual mission—also face that judgment. But always there is Jesus' offer of forgiveness and reconciliation when one realizes that he has been rejecting God and repents!

Matthew 11:20-24; 10:5-15

Where and in what forms do you today see the wickedness of Tyre and Sidon, Sodom and Gomorrah, and Capernaum?

You brood of vipers!
how can you speak good, when you are evil?

Matthew 12:34

Judgment should never be taken lightly. Jesus used extremely strong words to underscore its awful reality: "I tell you, on the day of judgment men will render account for every careless word they utter; for by your words you will be justified, and by your words you will be condemned." They were addressed to the Pharisees who had accused Jesus of casting out demons in the name of Satan. In speaking against the power of God's Holy Spirit, the Pharisees were actually rejecting the grace of God. Jesus condemned them with a powerful question: "You brood of vipers! how can you speak good, when you are evil? For out of the abundance of the heart the mouth speaks. The good man out of his good treasure brings forth good, and the evil man out of his evil treasure brings forth evil."

The abundance of the heart, the good treasure of the good man, refers to the Holy Spirit, the Counselor, the Comforter sent by Jesus from the Father.

Words are the expression of the inner nature, a person's soul. There are disciples who share their abundant treasure of God's grace with those whose lives they touch. They share words of forgiveness and reconciliation and of the peace that passes all understanding; reassuring words to help accomplish what may seem impossible tasks in one's special, unique mission; loving words to bring hope to those who are unloved; comforting words to heal the sorrow of emotional turmoil, physical illness, and the terrible depths of mourning; teaching words which can transform a seemingly ordinary passage into spiritual enlightenment; encouraging words which are vehicles of God's Spirit witnessing to His creative power and grace; compassionate words which speak to the soul's yearning for God.

Matthew 12:34-37; Luke 6:43-45

What does "evil" mean to you in the context of Jesus' question?

You serpents, you brood of vipers, how are you to escape being sentenced to hell?

Matthew 23:33

The Pharisees and scribes had gone too far in their cunning efforts to trick Jesus with their devious questions. In exasperation and indignation Jesus lashed out at them with a declamation of their shortcomings. His question is violent—it is a sentence of judgment.

What was the indictment? In their outward affectations and their strict observance of trifles and details of the law, they had lost sight of their mission to declare and display God's love. They wore bigger and bigger phylacteries—little leather boxes which contained scrolls of Bible verses—on forehead and wrist. The tassels on their robes had become ostentatious. The things which were to remind them and their people of God's infinite love and His promises of hope and salvation had become an outward show of piety to draw attention to themselves. They demanded the best seats in the synagogue, those facing the worshipers, so it could be seen how pious and religious they were. Their tithes of mint, dill, and cummin were meaningless. These were not crops but kitchen herbs, usually only one or two plants. They were like white-washed tombs—clean on the outside but full of death and decay inside. They cleansed the outside of their household cooking utensils. They paid more attention to outward cleanliness than inward forgiveness and love. They neglected justice; they did not show mercy; they did not reflect God's love and compassion, nor did they share their faith and the knowledge of God. They murdered the prophets—just as they would have a part in putting Jesus to death.

Lest we begin to feel superior to those Pharisees of long ago, it is necessary to examine ourselves. The Pharisees are no different than many people in the church everywhere throughout the ages! If we are to escape the sentence of hell, we must examine ourselves for hypocrisy. "If we say we have no sin, we deceive ourselves, and the truth is not in us. If we confess our sins, He is faithful and just, and will forgive our sins and cleanse us from all unrighteousness."

Matthew 23:5-6, 23-36; Luke 11:37-54; 1 John 1:8-10

How might we be subject to the same judgment as the Pharisees? How can we be clean on the inside as well as the outside? What can be done about the "natural man" or "old Adam"?

Do you see these great buildings?

Mark 13:1

Jesus had been teaching great crowds of people in the temple. The Temple of Herod was large and imposing, built with a wealth of grandeur and magnificence. As they were leaving, His disciples pointed out the buildings to Jesus, "Look, Teacher, what wonderful stones and what wonderful buildings."

Jesus' answer, "Do you see these great buildings? There will not be left here one stone upon another, that will not be thrown down," was a prophecy of the destruction of the temple by Rome in A.D. 70. But Jesus was referring to more than the physical destruction of the temple. He was referring to more than stones that would "be thrown down."

"O Jerusalem, Jerusalem, killing the prophets and stoning those who are sent to you! How often would I have gathered your children together as a hen gathers her brood under her wings, and you would not! Behold, your house is forsaken and desolate." Jesus' last words to the crowds before His passion are filled with profound sorrow and pathos. "House" can mean Israel, Jerusalem, or the temple—or all three. Jerusalem had a long history of rejecting the prophets, and therefore God. Now the Prophet who stood in the temple before them would also be rejected and despised.

The temple, the symbol of God's presence among His people, would be destroyed forever. God's kingdom would be carried by faithful disciples to all humankind. It would exist in the heart of each person who repented and followed Jesus. "Do you not know that you are God's temple and that God's Spirit dwells in you? If anyone destroys God's temple, God will destroy him. For God's temple is holy, and that temple you are."

God does not seek judgment on these temples, His beloved children. But the judgment which Israel, Jerusalem, and the temple saw, although accomplished by God through the destructive acts of man, is still frightening today. God commands obedience to His will. Only repentant sinners can escape His judgment.

Mark 13:1-2; Matthew 23:37—24:2, Luke 21:5-6; 1 Corinthians 3:16-17

Do you see anything in the church today that resembles the false practices of those who worshiped in the temple? How important are church buildings? How much should we spend on them?

Do you think that these Galileans were worse sinners than all the other Galileans, because they suffered thus? ... Or those eighteen upon whom the tower in Siloam fell and killed them, do you think that they were worse offenders than all the others who dwelt in Jerusalem?

Luke 13:2, 4

It was a widespread belief that all suffering and misfortune was the consequence of sinning. With these questions Jesus rejected that concept.

Natural disasters have always occurred throughout the entire world—earthquakes, torrential rains and floods, lightning-caused fires, hurricanes and tornadoes. There are disasters directly related to the ignorance and perfidy of people—floods from poorly engineered and constructed dams, fires in hotels which were not built with sufficient safeguards, nuclear radiation from faulty power plants run by insufficiently trained personnel, contamination of seafood, plants, and animals by carelessly stored chemical wastes, lung cancers in miners allowed to work without proper protection, bodily and property damage by persons driving under the influence of alcohol or other drugs, injury and death inflicted in the commission of crime, and the destruction of untold lives in meaningless wars. God does not single out the victims in such tragedies any more than the Galileans who died as the result of Pilate's corruption, or the 18 killed in Siloam. Natural disasters are part of our fallen creation. Human disasters are the result of greed, ignorance, dishonesty, vengeance, unscrupulousness, selfishness, pride, and lust of power.

The greatest disaster for the Jews was their rejection of Jesus as the Messiah. He came with the Gospel of love and forgiveness. In everything He taught and did He was showing the Israelites what their real mission was, and how it could be accomplished.

There is judgment today, tomorrow, and until the Second Advent for all those who refuse to give up their self-centered pride, who fail to repent, and who reject their role in discipleship. Harmony

140

with God, with oneself, with other people, and with the creation comes only to those who repent of their self-oriented pride, believe in Jesus as their Savior, and then follow Him in service to the world.

Luke 13:1-5; John 9:1-3

How do we interpret natural calamities in contrast to humanly caused disasters? What changes in values and behavior would have to take place to diminish or eliminate the latter?